# MAN CAVE FOOTBALL TRIVIA

## THE ULTIMATE COLLECTION OF PIGSKIN PUZZLERS

———— • ————

by

Jeff Kreismer

RED-LETTER PRESS, INC.
Saddle River, New Jersey

MAN CAVE FOOTBALL TRIVIA
Revised and Updated 2020
COPYRIGHT ©2014 Red-Letter Press, Inc.
ISBN: 9781603871709

Red-Letter Press, Inc.
P.O. Box 393
Saddle River, NJ 07458

www.Red-LetterPress.com

# ACKNOWLEDGMENTS

EDITORIAL:
Jack Kreismer

•

BOOK DESIGN & TYPOGRAPHY:
Jeff Kreismer

•

COVER & INTERIOR ART:
Andrew Towl

•

RESEARCH & DEVELOPMENT:
Kobus Reyneke
Mike Ryan

# MAN CAVE FOOTBALL TRIVIA

## THE ULTIMATE COLLECTION OF PIGSKIN PUZZLERS

# First Down

1. In their win over the Chiefs, what unlikely Packer scored the first touchdown in the history of the Super Bowl?

a) Bob Long
b) Max McGee
c) Don Chandler

2. In Cleveland's 1994 season opener, Tom Tupa cemented his name in the NFL history books by becoming the first player ever to…

a) Score on a two-point conversion
b) Miss six field goals in a single game
c) Record a safety on his team's first play of the season

3. Kyler Murray was the first pick of the 2019 NFL Draft, chosen by the Cardinals. He was also a first round pick of what baseball team in 2018?

a) Milwaukee Brewers
b) Cincinnati Reds
c) Oakland Athletics

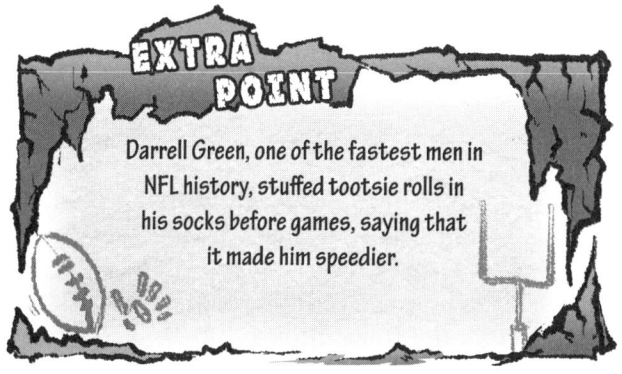

**EXTRA POINT**

Darrell Green, one of the fastest men in NFL history, stuffed tootsie rolls in his socks before games, saying that it made him speedier.

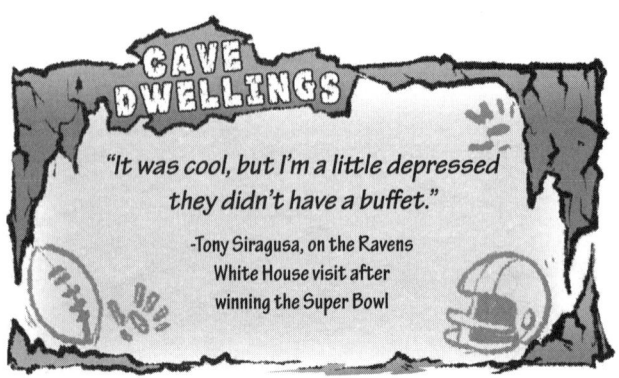

CAVE DWELLINGS

*"It was cool, but I'm a little depressed they didn't have a buffet."*

-Tony Siragusa, on the Ravens White House visit after winning the Super Bowl

4. What team was the first in NFL history to lose a Super Bowl in four different decades?

a) New York Giants
b) Pittsburgh Steelers
c) New England Patriots

5. What Browns Hall of Famer became the NFL's first black general manager with the Ravens in 2002?

a) Ozzie Newsome
b) Paul Warfield
c) Leroy Kelly

Answers: 1.B 2.A 3.C 4.C 5.A

# By the Numbers

1. In 2000, the Ravens set a 16-game single-season NFL record for points allowed. How many did they give up?

a) 165
b) 195
c) 215

2. In 2005, what #92 became the first player in NFL history to have his number officially retired by two teams?

a) Bruce Smith
b) Jerome Brown
c) Reggie White

3. When Jerry Rice joined the Seahawks in 2004, Steve Largent agreed to "unretire" his jersey number, as it was the same as the NFL's all-time leading receiver. What was it?

a) 80
b) 84
c) 88

**EXTRA POINT**

Hypothetically, if every single NFL team finished the regular season in a tie, the playoffs would be determined by a coin flip.

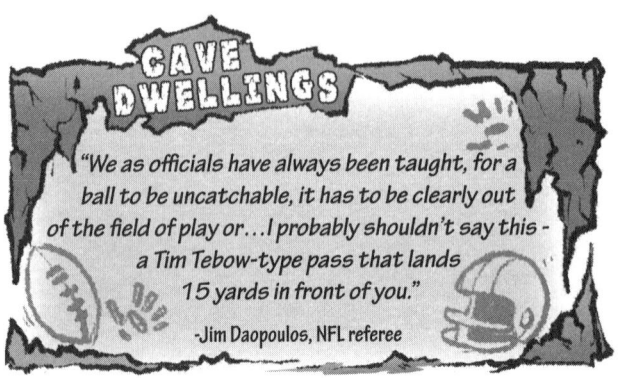

*"We as officials have always been taught, for a ball to be uncatchable, it has to be clearly out of the field of play or...I probably shouldn't say this - a Tim Tebow-type pass that lands 15 yards in front of you."*

-Jim Daopoulos, NFL referee

4. In 2013, Peyton Manning and Nick Foles both tied an NFL record by throwing how many touchdown passes in a single game?

a) 6
b) 7
c) 8

5. What NFL team has retired the #12 in honor of their fans, "The 12th Man"?

a) Seattle Seahawks
b) Pittsburgh Steelers
c) Denver Broncos

Answers: 1.A 2.C (with the Eagles and Packers) 3.A 4.B 5.A

# Return on Investment

1. What Bear made NFL history in 2001 with back-to-back overtime interception returns for scores to beat the 49ers and Browns in consecutive weeks?

a) Mike Brown
b) R.W. McQuarters
c) Charles Tillman

2. Who set the record for the longest kickoff return in NFL history, 109 yards, in 2013?

a) Josh Cribbs
b) Cordarrelle Patterson
c) Jacoby Jones

3. What player set an NFL record in 2003 when he returned a kickoff or punt for a touchdown in four consecutive games?

a) Brian Mitchell
b) Dante Hall
c) Devin Hester

**EXTRA POINT**

During the 1958 Colts-Giants NFL Championship Game, an employee of NBC posed as a fan and ran onto the field to delay the game because the national television feed went dead.

CAVE DWELLINGS

*"A lot, 'cause I'm drunk..."*

-Pat McAfee, Colts punter, after police
found him taking an early morning swim
in a canal and asked him
how much he had to drink

4. In 1997, who became the first NFL player to score touchdowns on an interception return, fumble return and kickoff return in the same season?

a) Mel Gray
b) Deion Sanders
c) Rodney Harrison

5. In 2012, what two Bears became the first teammates in NFL history to each return an interception for a TD in consecutive games?

a) Brian Urlacher and Tim Jennings
b) Julius Peppers and Chris Conte
c) Charles Tillman and Lance Briggs

Answers: 1.A 2.B 3.B 4.C 5.C

# Three's Company

1. What team, that won only 14 games from 2008-10, managed to defeat the defending Super Bowl champs (Giants, Steelers and Saints) in each of those three seasons?

a) Jacksonville Jaguars
b) Oakland Raiders
c) Cleveland Browns

2. Who is the only player in NFL history to gain 4,000 yards three different ways-rushing, receiving, and on kickoff returns?

a) Herschel Walker
b) Brian Westbrook
c) Tiki Barber

3. The first running back in NFL history to have 1,000-yard seasons for three different teams began his career with San Francisco. Who is he?

a) Ricky Watters
b) Garrison Hearst
c) Charlie Garner

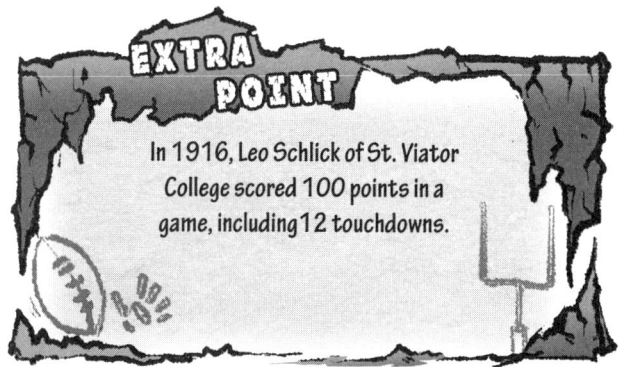

**EXTRA POINT**

In 1916, Leo Schlick of St. Viator College scored 100 points in a game, including 12 touchdowns.

"I really don't like water. I'm trying.
I really just don't like it."

-Odell Beckham Jr., on leaving
a game due to dehydration

4. What rookie scored the first three TDs of his NFL career all in one quarter in 2011?

a) A.J. Green
b) Torrey Smith
c) Jeremy Kerley

5. After winning the previous two Super Bowls as a Cowboy, what player became the first to win three in a row after beating San Diego as a member of the 49ers?

a) Ken Norton, Jr.
b) Charles Haley
c) Deion Sanders

Answers: 1.C 2.A 3.A (The Eagles and Seahawks are the other two teams.) 4.B 5.A

# School Days

1. At Oklahoma State, Barry Sanders played in the same backfield with what fellow future Hall of Fame runner?

a) Marcus Allen
b) Emmitt Smith
c) Thurman Thomas

2. What NFL All-Pro runner was the first player in college football history at any level to have 1,000 yards rushing and 1,000 receiving in the same season in 1998?

a) Brian Westbrook
b) Edgerrin James
c) LaDainian Tomlinson

3. At what small school did Jerry Rice break numerous NCAA Division I-AA records?

a) Mississippi Valley State
b) Appalachian State
c) North Dakota State

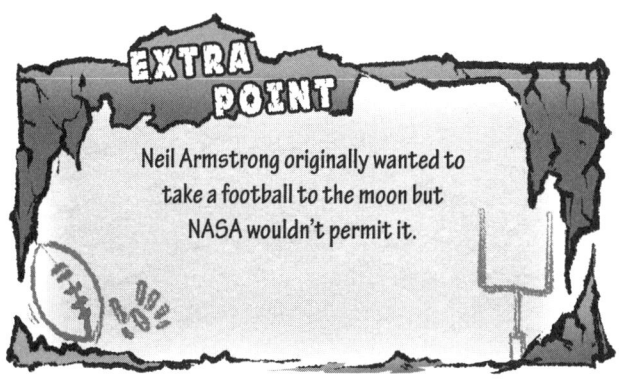

**EXTRA POINT**

Neil Armstrong originally wanted to take a football to the moon but NASA wouldn't permit it.

"I'm traveling to all 51 states
to see who can stop 85."

-Chad Johnson

4. Tom Brady's final game at the University of Michigan was a thriller. He threw four TDs as the Wolverines beat Alabama in overtime, 35-34, in what 2000 bowl game?

a) Fiesta Bowl
b) Orange Bowl
c) Rose Bowl

5. What two sack artists attended Auburn High School together in Alabama before they were teammates at Troy University?

a) DeMarcus Ware and Osi Umenyiora
b) J.J. Watt and Von Miller
c) Jared Allen and Shawne Merriman

Answers:  1.C 2.A (at Villanova) 3.A 4.B 5.A

# Record Breakers

1. In 2002, who set an NFL record by scoring five first half touchdowns in a game between the Seahawks and Vikings?

a) Robert Smith
b) Randy Moss
c) Shaun Alexander

2. Against Seattle in 1986, what Jet became the first player in NFL history to throw for over 400 yards in a game and earn a perfect quarterback rating of 158.3?

a) Ken O'Brien
b) Richard Todd
c) Boomer Esiason

3. What linebacker set an NFL record with seven quarterback sacks in a single 1990 game?

a) Derrick Thomas
b) Lawrence Taylor
c) Pat Swilling

**EXTRA POINT**

The NFL is considered to be a non-profit organization by the IRS and, as such, is tax exempt.

## CAVE DWELLINGS

*"I know one thing about these guys. They're not going to stop quitting."*

-Chad Henne, NFL quarterback,
on the state of his team
following a loss

4. In 2018, who became the first quarterback to throw for at least 400 yards in three consecutive games?

a) Case Keenum
b) Ryan Fitzpatrick
c) Ryan Tannehill

5. What Redskin made NFL history by recording four interceptions in a single half of a 2010 game?

a) Carlos Rogers
b) DeAngelo Hall
c) Fred Smoot

Answers: 1.C 2.A 3.A 4.B 5.B

# Monday Night Football

1. In a 2009 *Monday Night Football* game, the Colts came out on top despite having the ball for just 14 minutes and 53 seconds. Who did they defeat, 27-23?

a) St. Louis Rams
b) Miami Dolphins
c) Tennessee Titans

2. In a 2005 "Monday Night Massacre," the Eagles were destroyed, 42-0, by what team?

a) Seattle Seahawks
b) Dallas Cowboys
c) Indianapolis Colts

3. In 2003, the day after his father's death, Brett Favre put on an inspiring performance on *MNF* as the Packers blew out what team 41-7?

a) Denver Broncos
b) Oakland Raiders
c) Kansas City Chiefs

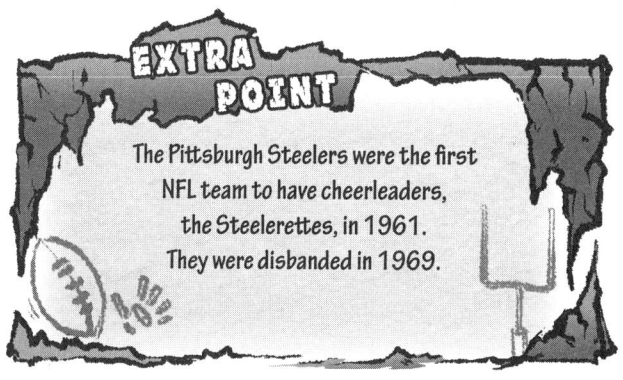

**EXTRA POINT**

The Pittsburgh Steelers were the first NFL team to have cheerleaders, the Steelerettes, in 1961. They were disbanded in 1969.

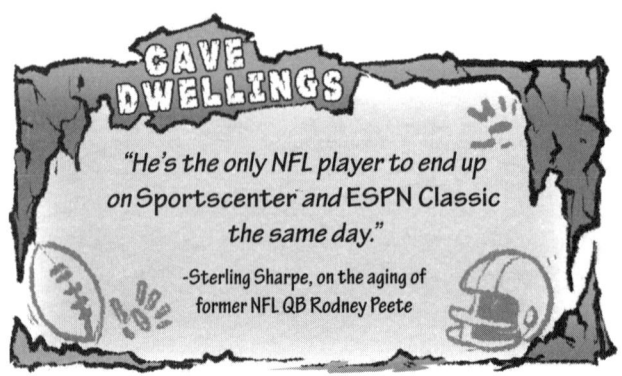

"He's the only NFL player to end up on Sportscenter and ESPN Classic the same day."

-Sterling Sharpe, on the aging of former NFL QB Rodney Peete

4. In a 2018 *MNF* classic, the Chiefs put up 51 points, the most ever scored in a game by a losing team. Who topped them by scoring 54?

a) New Orleans Saints
b) New England Patriots
c) Los Angeles Rams

5. What two teams took part in the very first *Monday Night Football* game in 1970?

a) Browns and Jets
b) Giants and Cowboys
c) Patriots and Broncos

Answers: 1.B 2.A 3.B 4.C 5.A (Cleveland won, 31-21.)

# Who Am I?

1. As a teenager, I was a ball boy for the Vikings. In 2005, I had my first 1,000-yard receiving season in the NFL.

a) Andre Johnson
b) Braylon Edwards
c) Larry Fitzgerald

2. Years after I scored the first touchdown in Seahawks Super Bowl history, I married women's professional soccer goalie Hope Solo in 2012.

a) Mack Strong
b) Jerramy Stevens
c) Joe Jurevicius

3. Before I became the first pure placekicker in the Pro Football Hall of Fame, I scored the first nine points of Super Bowl IV for the Chiefs.

a) Nick Lowery
b) Jim Turner
c) Jan Stenerud

**EXTRA POINT**

Minimum pay for a rookie in the NFL is $495,000.

**CAVE DWELLINGS**

*"Now I'm completing up the other half of that triangle."*

-Emmitt Smith, on joining teammates
Michael Irvin and Troy Aikman
in the Hall of Fame

4. In 2009, my fourth season in Cleveland, I ran for 286 yards and three touchdowns in a game against the Chiefs. Before that, I hadn't even surpassed 250 in an entire season.

a) Jerome Harrison
b) Peyton Hillis
c) William Green

5. I have the most wins of any NFL head coach that has never won a Super Bowl.

a) Dan Reeves
b) Marty Schottenheimer
c) Jeff Fisher

Answers: 1.C 2.B 3.C 4.A 5.B

# Two of a Kind

1. In 2008, who became the first-ever coach/QB combo to win their NFL debut together?

a) Rex Ryan and Mark Sanchez (Jets)
b) John Harbaugh and Joe Flacco (Ravens)
c) Ron Rivera and Cam Newton (Panthers)

2. The year 1979 brought together two legends on the same team– one in his final NFL season and the other a rookie. Which of the pairs is it?

a) Bart Starr and James Lofton (Packers)
b) Fran Tarkenton and Lawrence Taylor (Giants)
c) O.J. Simpson and Joe Montana (49ers)

3. Who was the first father-son QB duo to each be on a Super Bowl championship team?

a) Bob and Brian Griese
b) Phil and Chris Simms
c) Don and Matt Hasselbeck

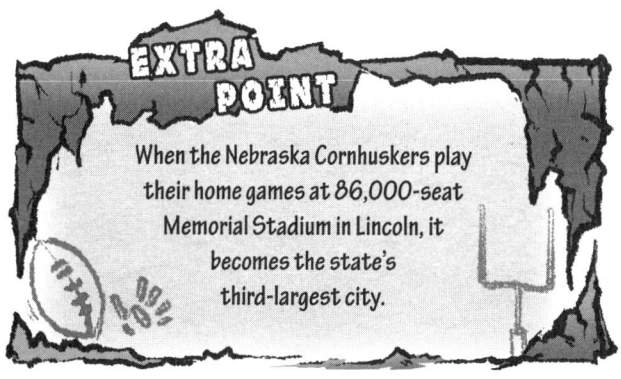

**EXTRA POINT**

When the Nebraska Cornhuskers play their home games at 86,000-seat Memorial Stadium in Lincoln, it becomes the state's third-largest city.

"I tried to win it so we could get Le'Veon (Bell) back. It didn't work."

-JuJu Smith Schuster, on buying 100+ Mega Millions tickets to help his Steelers keep their former star

4. What two players in NFL history have run for over 5,000 yards with two different teams?

a) Corey Dillon and Warrick Dunn
b) Jerome Bettis and Marcus Allen
c) Eric Dickerson and Marshall Faulk

5. Armed with the #1 overall pick in both 1999 and 2000, what team ended up drafting two busts in back-to-back years?

a) Cincinnati Bengals
b) Cleveland Browns
c) Houston Texans

Answers: 1.B 2.C 3.A (with the Dolphins and Broncos, respectively) 4.C (Both did it with the Colts and Rams.) 5.B (Tim Couch and Courtney Brown)

# The Award Goes To...

1. In 2001, who became the first NFL player to be named the Comeback Player of the Year twice?

a) Garrison Hearst
b) Jerry Rice
c) Doug Flutie

2. Who was named the NFL's Defensive Rookie of the Year in 2012 and the Defensive Player of the Year in 2013?

a) Von Miller
b) Luke Kuechly
c) Sheldon Richardson

3. Thanks to a 2004 game in which the Chiefs scored eight rushing TDs vs. the Falcons, who became the first offensive lineman ever named the AFC Offensive Player of the Week?

a) Brian Waters
b) Willie Roaf
c) Will Shields

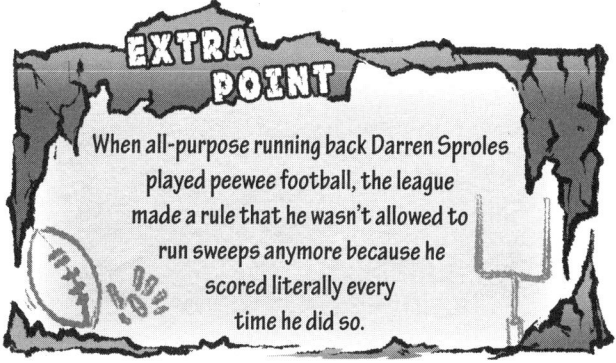

**EXTRA POINT**

When all-purpose running back Darren Sproles played peewee football, the league made a rule that he wasn't allowed to run sweeps anymore because he scored literally every time he did so.

*"Pain is only temporary,
no matter how long it lasts."*

-Ray Lewis

4. What QB was the MVP of the 1978 Rose Bowl, the 1997 Pro Bowl, and is a member of the Canadian and Pro Football Halls of Fame?

a) Steve Young
b) Vinny Testaverde
c) Warren Moon

5. In their defeat to the Baltimore Colts, what Cowboy became the first defensive player, and the first from a losing team, to be named the Super Bowl MVP?

a) Cliff Harris
b) Herb Adderley
c) Chuck Howley

Answers: 1.A 2.B 3.A 4.C 5.C

# Sack Attack

1. Who holds the record for the most career sacks in the NFL postseason with 16?

a) Dwight Freeney
b) Willie McGinest
c) Reggie White

2. What future NFL head coach did Ray Lewis record his first NFL sack against when his Ravens played the Colts in 1996?

a) Gary Kubiak
b) Jason Garrett
c) Jim Harbaugh

3. With an even 200 QB takedowns, who is the NFL's all-time leader in sacks?

a) Bruce Smith
b) Michael Strahan
c) Reggie White

**EXTRA POINT**

Hall of Fame quarterback Troy Aikman was born with a clubfoot and wore special shoes until he was three.

**CAVE DWELLINGS**

*"He meant everything he was saying, but I didn't know what he was talking about 90 percent of the time."*

-Joe Flacco, on Ray Lewis' pre-game speeches

4. What Bears Hall of Famer had back-to-back 17-sack seasons and led the NFL in the category in 1985?

a) William Perry
b) Richard Dent
c) Steve McMichael

5. What team sacked Jay Cutler nine times in the first half in an embarrassing 2010 Chicago defeat?

a) New York Giants
b) Green Bay Packers
c) New Orleans Saints

Answers: 1.B 2.C 3.A 4.B 5.A

# Go Long

1. At 96 yards, who provided the longest overtime rushing touchdown in NFL history in 1998 to send his team to victory over the Jets in their season opener?

a) Lawrence Phillips
b) Garrison Hearst
c) Terrell Davis

2. Set in 2013, who holds the NFL record for the longest touchdown run by a quarterback, at 93 yards?

a) Terrelle Pryor
b) Colin Kaepernick
c) Austin Davis

3. In 2011, who returned a kickoff 104 yards to the opponents' 3-yard line to set a new mark for the longest non-scoring play in NFL history?

a) Devin Hester
b) Percy Harvin
c) Leon Washington

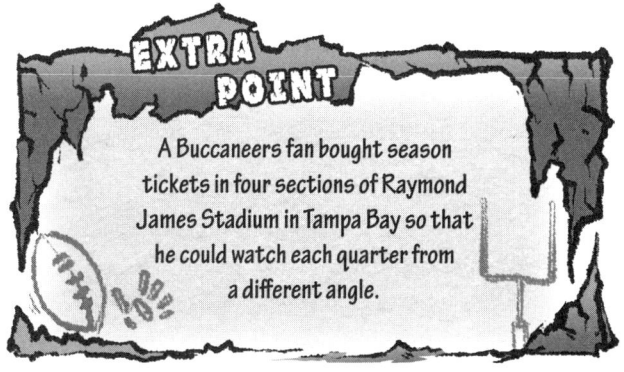

EXTRA POINT

A Buccaneers fan bought season tickets in four sections of Raymond James Stadium in Tampa Bay so that he could watch each quarter from a different angle.

"On this team we are all united in a common goal: to keep my job."

-Lou Holtz

4. In 2018, who joined Tony Dorsett when he became the second NFL player to run for a 99-yard touchdown?

a) Derrick Henry
b) Joe Mixon
c) Nick Chubb

5. In one 2007 contest, two players made NFL history with yardage records. Adrian Peterson ran for 296 yards while what opponent returned a missed field goal 109 yards for a TD?

a) Antonio Cromartie
b) Devin Hester
c) Dante Hall

# The One and Only

1. What team handed the legendary Vince Lombardi the only postseason defeat of his career by beating his Packers in the 1960 NFL Championship Game?

a) Philadelphia Eagles
b) Washington Redskins
c) New York Giants

2. Only one player has posted a perfect 158.3 quarterback rating in his first NFL regular season game. Who?

a) Blake Bortles
b) Marcus Mariota
c) Derek Carr

3. Who is the only man to be the head coach of both the Baltimore Colts and Baltimore Ravens?

a) Lindy Infante
b) Brian Billick
c) Ted Marchibroda

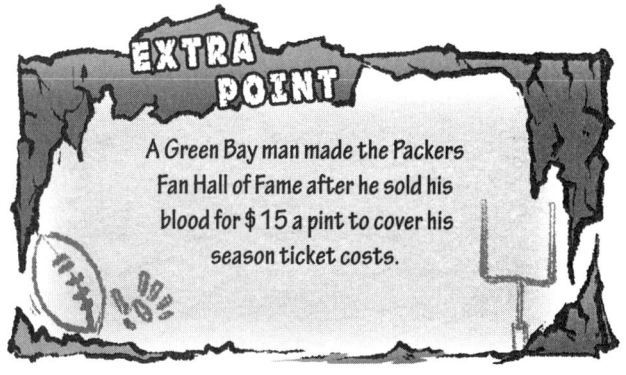

**EXTRA POINT**

A Green Bay man made the Packers Fan Hall of Fame after he sold his blood for $15 a pint to cover his season ticket costs.

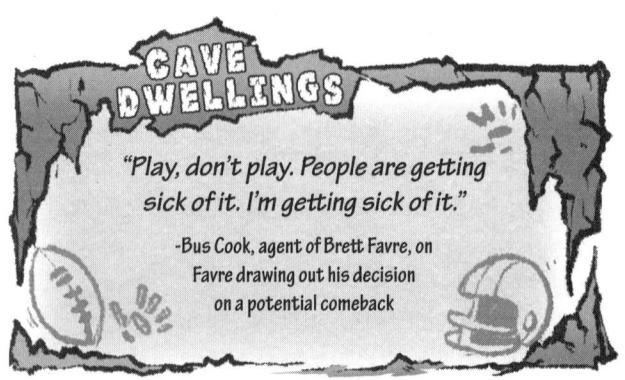

**CAVE DWELLINGS**

*"Play, don't play. People are getting sick of it. I'm getting sick of it."*

-Bus Cook, agent of Brett Favre, on Favre drawing out his decision on a potential comeback

4. What speedster remains the only person to win an individual Olympic gold medal and a Super Bowl ring?

a) Carl Lewis
b) Bob Hayes
c) James Jett

5. What is the only team in NFL history to play in both the AFC and NFC Championship Games?

a) Seattle Seahawks
b) St. Louis/Arizona Cardinals
c) Tampa Bay Buccaneers

Answers: 1.A 2.B 3.C 4.B (with the Cowboys) 5.A

# Playoff Puzzlers

1. As the head coach of the Cleveland Browns, Bill Belichick won his first career playoff game against what team in 1994?

a) Pittsburgh Steelers
b) New England Patriots
c) New York Jets

2. What Packer ended Seattle's 2003 season when he recorded the first defensive touchdown in a playoff overtime game in NFL history?

a) Bhawoh Jue
b) Mike McKenzie
c) Al Harris

3. The Lions have won only one postseason contest since their 1957 NFL championship victory. Who did they defeat in the 1991 Playoffs?

a) Dallas Cowboys
b) New Orleans Saints
c) Green Bay Packers

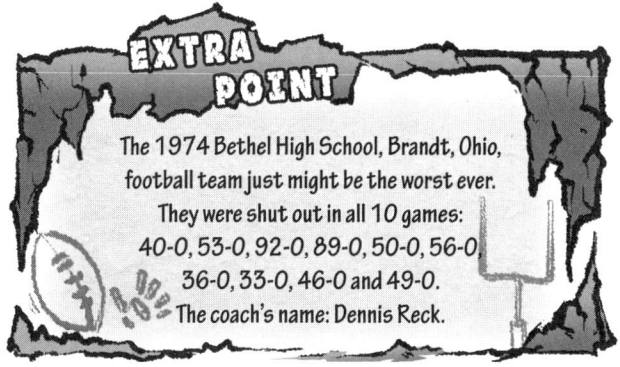

**EXTRA POINT**

The 1974 Bethel High School, Brandt, Ohio, football team just might be the worst ever. They were shut out in all 10 games: 40-0, 53-0, 92-0, 89-0, 50-0, 56-0, 36-0, 33-0, 46-0 and 49-0. The coach's name: Dennis Reck.

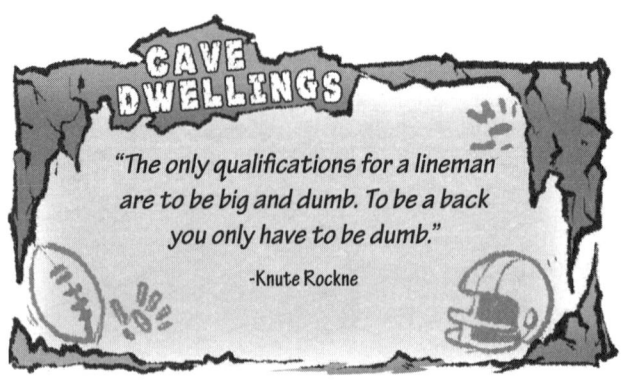

**CAVE DWELLINGS**

*"The only qualifications for a lineman are to be big and dumb. To be a back you only have to be dumb."*

-Knute Rockne

4. The Bears defeated the Eagles in their 1988 Divisional Playoff contest that became known by what name because of the extreme weather conditions at Soldier Field?

a) Snow Bowl
b) Fog Bowl
c) Ice Bowl

5. What team's heartbreaking last-second loss in the 2015 postseason marked their eighth consecutive playoff defeat?

a) Washington Redskins
b) Minnesota Vikings
c) Cincinnati Bengals

Answers: 1.B 2.C 3.A 4.B 5.C (They lost to the Steelers.)

# Multi-Sport Stars

1. Who was the first person to play in both a World Series and a Super Bowl (XXIX)?

a) Brian Jordan
b) Deion Sanders
c) Bo Jackson

2. In addition to football, Tony Gonzalez was a basketball player who took part in the 1997 Sweet Sixteen of the NCAA Tournament for what school?

a) Texas
b) Florida
c) California

3. Colin Kaepernick was selected in the 43rd round of the 2009 Major League Baseball Draft by what team?

a) Chicago Cubs
b) New York Yankees
c) Detroit Tigers

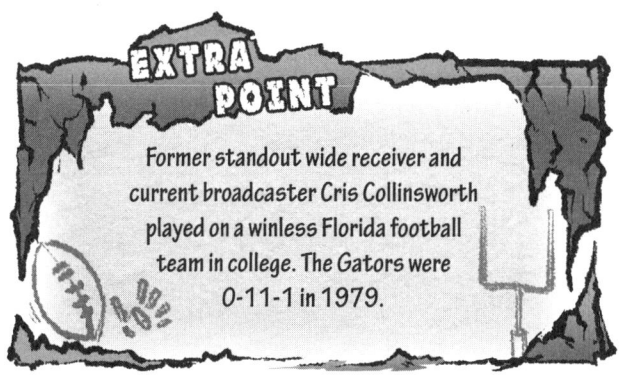

**EXTRA POINT**

Former standout wide receiver and current broadcaster Cris Collinsworth played on a winless Florida football team in college. The Gators were 0-11-1 in 1979.

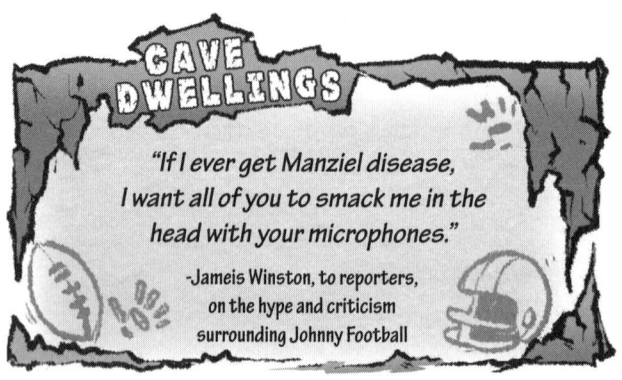

*"If I ever get Manziel disease, I want all of you to smack me in the head with your microphones."*

-Jameis Winston, to reporters, on the hype and criticism surrounding Johnny Football

4. As a member of the 1984 49ers, what Pro Bowl lineman and shot putter is the only athlete to win both a Super Bowl ring and an Olympic medal within a year's time?

a) Charles Haley
b) Michael Carter
c) Fred Dean

5. Who is the only man ever to coach a team in the Super Bowl (Vikings) and play on a title team in the NBA (1950 Minneapolis Lakers)?

a) Bud Grant
b) Jerry Burns
c) Norm Van Brocklin

Answers: 1.B (with the 49ers) 2.C 3.A 4.B 5.A

# Draft Day

1. Who was the last running back to be selected #1 overall in the NFL Draft?

a) Bo Jackson
b) Ki-Jana Carter
c) Reggie Bush

2. Who became the first pick in the history of the Ravens when Baltimore selected him #4 overall in the 1996 NFL Draft?

a) Jonathan Ogden
b) Ray Lewis
c) Ed Reed

3. Arguably the biggest draft bust ever, who was tabbed by *Sports Illustrated* as "the best offensive line prospect ever" before Green Bay took him #2 in 1989?

a) Jim Dombrowski
b) Antone Davis
c) Tony Mandarich

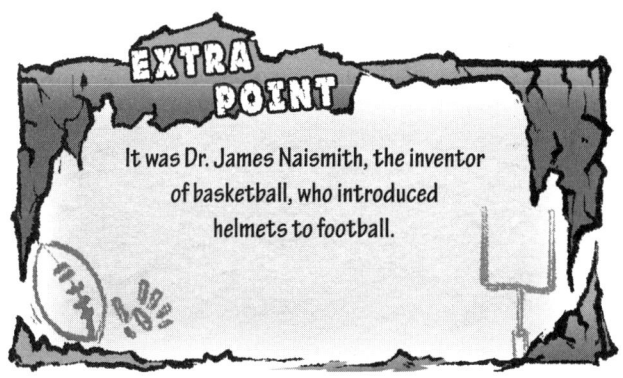

**EXTRA POINT**

It was Dr. James Naismith, the inventor of basketball, who introduced helmets to football.

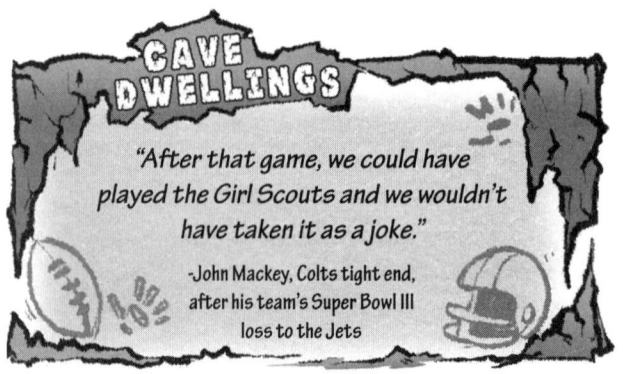

CAVE DWELLINGS

*"After that game, we could have played the Girl Scouts and we wouldn't have taken it as a joke."*

-John Mackey, Colts tight end, after his team's Super Bowl III loss to the Jets

4. Joe Namath elected to sign with the AFL's Jets after what NFL team also drafted him in 1965?

a) Green Bay Packers
b) St. Louis Cardinals
c) San Francisco 49ers

5. In 2014, what team selected Michael Sam with their seventh round pick, making him the first openly gay player to be drafted into the NFL?

a) New York Jets
b) Dallas Cowboys
c) St. Louis Rams

# The Agony of Defeat

1. In 1999, the Jacksonville Jaguars finished the season 15-3 (counting playoff games). All three losses came to the same team. Who?

a) Pittsburgh Steelers
b) Tennessee Titans
c) Indianapolis Colts

2. What team began NFL play in 1976 and went on to lose their first 26 games?

a) Atlanta Falcons
b) New Orleans Saints
c) Tampa Bay Buccaneers

3. In 2003, the Packers lost a playoff game for the first time ever at Lambeau Field. Who beat them 27-7?

a) Washington Redskins
b) Atlanta Falcons
c) Minnesota Vikings

**EXTRA POINT**

The Campbell's Soup red and white label was inspired by the colors of the Cornell University football team.

"Because John McEnroe
never played it."

-Larry Felser, sports columnist,
on why so many people
love pro football

4. What team was on the wrong side of NFL
history when it became the first to lose a playoff
game to a club with a losing record in 2011?

a) Carolina Panthers
b) New Orleans Saints
c) Chicago Bears

5. What team lost to the expansion Texans in
Houston's first-ever NFL game in 2002?

a) Dallas Cowboys
b) Green Bay Packers
c) San Francisco 49ers

Answers: 1.B 2.C 3.B 4.B (They lost to the 7-9
Seahawks.) 5.A

# Presidential

1. When former AFL quarterback Jack Kemp ran for Vice-President of the United States in 1996, who was the presidential candidate on his ticket?

a) Ross Perot
b) Bob Dole
c) Michael Dukakis

2. What United States Football League team did Donald Trump own during the 1980s?

a) Tampa Bay Bandits
b) New Jersey Generals
c) Houston Gamblers

3. What president was credited with radically changing the rules of American football and introducing the forward pass in 1906?

a) Theodore Roosevelt
b) Woodrow Wilson
c) Grover Cleveland

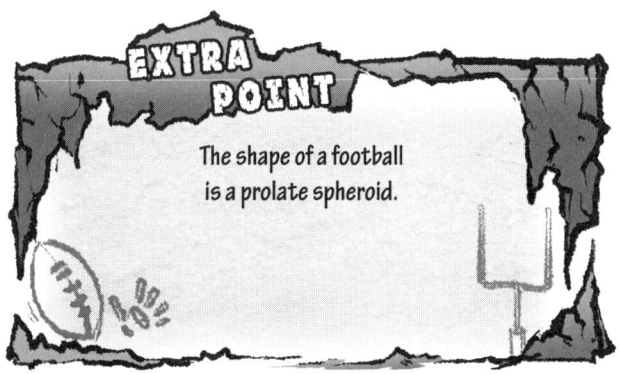

**EXTRA POINT**

The shape of a football is a prolate spheroid.

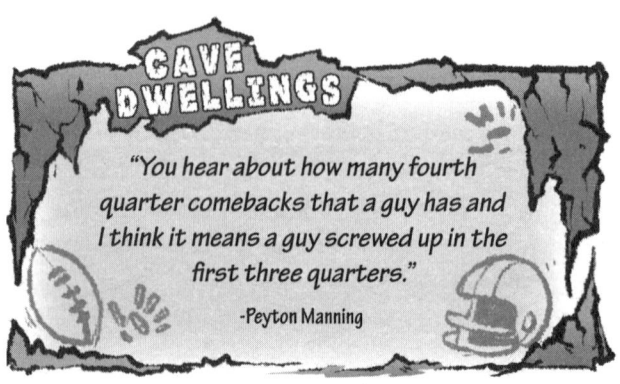

**CAVE DWELLINGS**

*"You hear about how many fourth quarter comebacks that a guy has and I think it means a guy screwed up in the first three quarters."*

-Peyton Manning

4. President Gerald Ford was a center on what 1932 and '33 national championship college team?

a) USC
b) Princeton
c) Michigan

5. In 1969, Richard Nixon declared this team the national champions over an undefeated Penn State squad.

a) Georgia
b) Oklahoma
c) Texas

Answers: 1.B 2.B 3.A 4.C 5.C

# Sweet Sixteen

1. The 16 combined points in Super Bowl LIII, won by the Patriots over the Rams, was the lowest total in the game's history. How many points did the Pats score?

a) 10
b) 13
c) 16

2. What Hall of Fame receiver played 16 NFL seasons and finished his career with the Rams and Eagles in 1993?

a) James Lofton
b) Henry Ellard
c) Steve Largent

3. In what year did the NFL move from a 14 to a 16 game regular season?

a) 1970
b) 1974
c) 1978

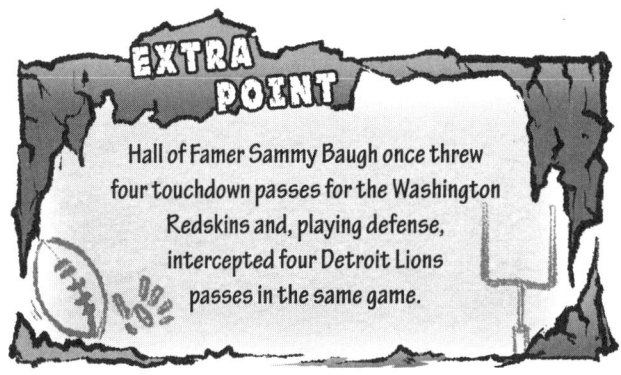

**EXTRA POINT**

Hall of Famer Sammy Baugh once threw four touchdown passes for the Washington Redskins and, playing defense, intercepted four Detroit Lions passes in the same game.

**CAVE DWELLINGS**

*"We have a lot of stars,
just no one you've ever heard of."*

-Tom Donahue, 49ers GM,
defending his team

4. Trailing 16-15 with 16 seconds left, the Titans pulled off their 2000 "Music City Miracle" over the Bills when what player took a Frank Wycheck lateral on the kickoff 75 yards for a TD?

a) Lorenzo Neal
b) Kevin Dyson
c) Derrick Mason

5. What #16 was the first overall pick of the 2016 NFL Draft?

a) Jameis Winston
b) Mitchell Trubisky
c) Jared Goff

Answers: 1.B 2.A 3.C 4.B 5.C

# Oh, Brother

1. Thanks to a 2018 trade, twins Devin and Jason McCourty were brought together to play on what team?

a) New England Patriots
b) Baltimore Ravens
c) Cleveland Browns

2. Super Bowl XLVIII MVP Malcolm Smith has a brother who made the 2009 Pro Bowl. What's his name?

a) Sean Smith
b) Steve Smith
c) Jimmy Smith

3. As a Viking, Eddie led the NFL in kick return yardage in 1980. His brother is a member of the Pro Football Hall of Fame. What's their last name?

a) Sanders
b) Sayers
c) Payton

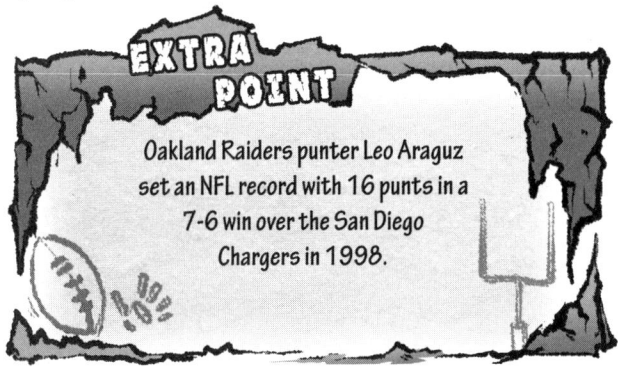

### EXTRA POINT

Oakland Raiders punter Leo Araguz set an NFL record with 16 punts in a 7-6 win over the San Diego Chargers in 1998.

**CAVE DWELLINGS**

*"I'd just like to put it behind me."*

-Peyton Manning, when asked about
the alleged "mooning" of teammates
in front of a female trainer

4. Two brothers of different last names were both Vikings in 2001. One was a Defensive Rookie of the Year as a Chief. The other had over 6,000 yards in Minnesota. Name them.

a) Dale Carter and Jake Reed
b) Kendrell Bell and Randy Moss
c) Neil Smith and Michael Bennett

5. What former NFL receiver's brother once served as the head coach of the NBA's Raptors?

a) Jerry Rice
b) Cris Carter
c) Marvin Harrison

Answers: 1.A 2.B (with the Giants) 3.C (Walter Payton is the Hall of Famer.) 4.A 5.B (brother Butch Carter)

# Let's Make a Deal

1. Along with their first round pick, what Pro Bowl center did the Seahawks trade to the Saints in 2015 to acquire Jimmy Graham?

a) Jahri Evans
b) Evan Mathis
c) Max Unger

2. In 1980, the Giants and 49ers swapped defensive backs who would both later become NFL head coaches. New York sent Ray Rhodes to San Francisco in return for what player?

a) John Harbaugh
b) Bill Cowher
c) Tony Dungy

3. In a rare swap of Pro Bowlers, who did the Washington Redskins receive when they sent Champ Bailey to the Broncos in 2004?

a) Clinton Portis
b) Stephen Davis
c) Mike Anderson

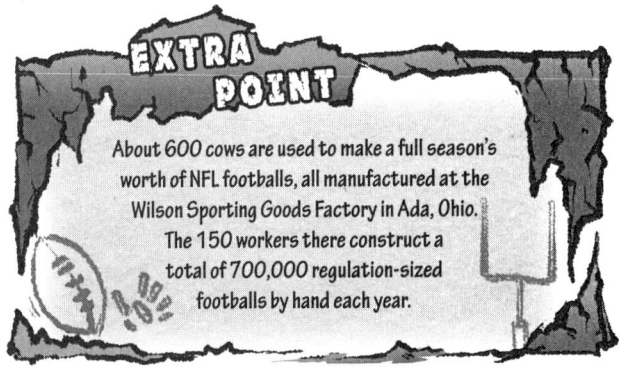

**EXTRA POINT**

About 600 cows are used to make a full season's worth of NFL footballs, all manufactured at the Wilson Sporting Goods Factory in Ada, Ohio. The 150 workers there construct a total of 700,000 regulation-sized footballs by hand each year.

*"There's two times of year for me: Football season, and waiting for football season."*

-Darius Rucker, musician

4. What team received a wealth of draft choices when they moved out of the #2 spot of the 2012 NFL Draft after the Redskins traded up to select Robert Griffin III?

a) Cleveland Browns
b) St. Louis Rams
c) Jacksonville Jaguars

5. In a lopsided NFL trade, the Cowboys received numerous franchise-building picks when they dealt Herschel Walker to what team in 1989?

a) Philadelphia Eagles
b) Minnesota Vikings
c) New York Jets

Answers: 1.C 2.C 3.A 4.B 5.B

# Just For Kicks

1. What Redskin became the first-ever special teamer to win the MVP award after the 1982 strike-shortened season?

a) Norm Johnson
b) Mark Moseley
c) Curt Knight

2. Who tied his own playoff record when he made five field goals and accounted for all of his team's points in a 15-6 win over the Ravens in the 2006 Playoffs?

a) Adam Vinatieri
b) Jason Elam
c) Nate Kaeding

3. Who holds the record for the longest field goal in NFL history at 64 yards?

a) Matt Prater
b) Tom Dempsey
c) Sebastian Janikowski

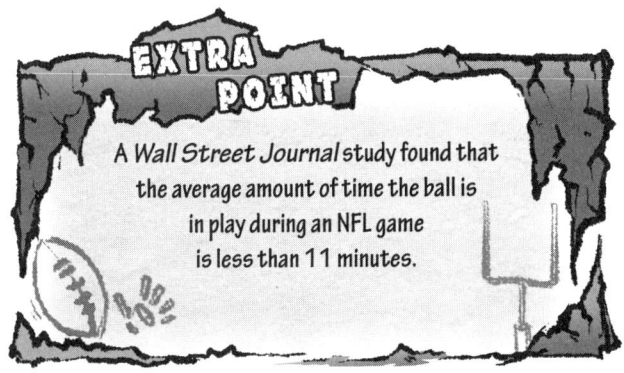

**EXTRA POINT**

A *Wall Street Journal* study found that the average amount of time the ball is in play during an NFL game is less than 11 minutes.

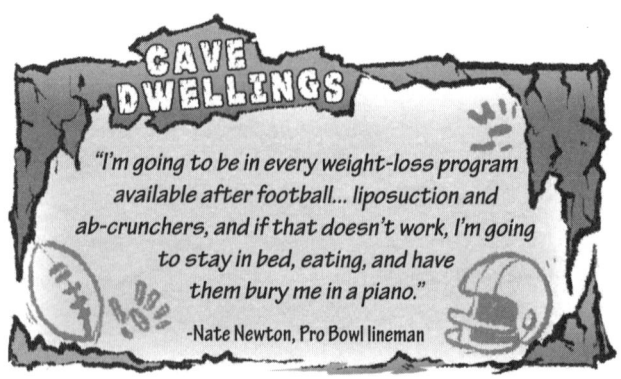

**CAVE DWELLINGS**

*"I'm going to be in every weight-loss program available after football... liposuction and ab-crunchers, and if that doesn't work, I'm going to stay in bed, eating, and have them bury me in a piano."*

-Nate Newton, Pro Bowl lineman

4. Whose missed 32-yard field goal would have tied the Ravens with the Patriots in the closing seconds of the 2011 AFC Championship Game?

a) Billy Cundiff
b) Matt Stover
c) Justin Tucker

5. In 2006, the (then) all-time leading scorer for the Packers accounted for all 16 Vikings points vs. the Panthers by kicking three field goals and throwing a 16-yard touchdown pass. Who is he?

a) Paul Edinger
b) Ryan Longwell
c) Chris Jacke

Answers: 1.B 2.A (with the Colts) 3.A (in 2013) 4.A 5.B

# Second in Command

1. As a backup at the University of Michigan, Tom Brady watched what future NFL QB lead the Wolverines to an undefeated 1997 season?

a) Brian Griese
b) Drew Henson
c) Chad Henne

2. What reserve quarterback led the biggest comeback in NFL playoff history when his Bills won, 41-38, after trailing the Oilers by 32 in the 1992 playoffs?

a) Todd Collins
b) Doug Flutie
c) Frank Reich

3. When Brett Favre first arrived in Green Bay, he briefly sat behind what Pro Bowl quarterback who would leave the Packers after the 1992 season?

a) Don Majkowski
b) Jim Everett
c) Mike Tomczak

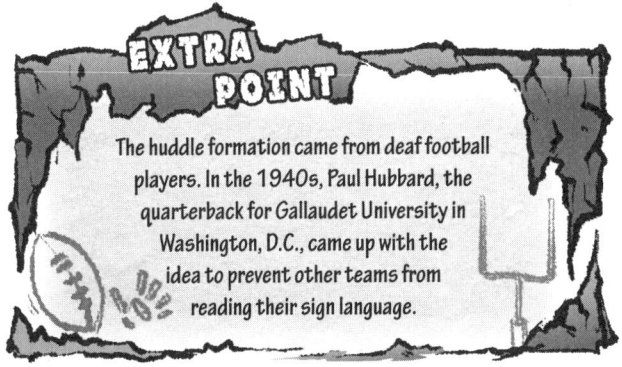

**EXTRA POINT**

The huddle formation came from deaf football players. In the 1940s, Paul Hubbard, the quarterback for Gallaudet University in Washington, D.C., came up with the idea to prevent other teams from reading their sign language.

**CAVE DWELLINGS**

*"I was kinda scared. I thought Detroit was gonna take me. I would've asked them for so much money they would have to put me on layaway."*

-Deion Sanders, on almost being drafted by the Lions

4. In the 2012 postseason, what Viking became the first quarterback in NFL history to start a playoff game after not having thrown a single pass during that year's regular season?

a) Christian Ponder
b) Joe Webb
c) Matt Cassel

5. Jim McMahon finished his NFL career with two Super Bowl rings- one with the Bears and another as a backup with what squad?

a) Dallas Cowboys
b) Green Bay Packers
c) San Francisco 49ers

Answers: 1.A 2.C 3.A 4.B 5.B

# Keeping Score

1. What's the score of a forfeited football game?

a) 2-0
b) 6-0
c) 14-0

2. The Eagles defeated the Giants in the 2008 postseason in the first-ever NFL game that finished with what score?

a) 3-2
b) 23-11
c) 37-19

3. A 51-45 Wild Card shootout in 2010 that ended in overtime set an NFL postseason record for total points. What two teams took part in it?

a) Cowboys and Eagles
b) Saints and Lions
c) Cardinals and Packers

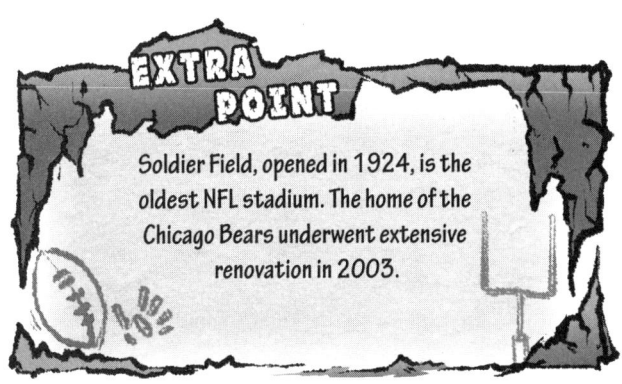

**EXTRA POINT**

Soldier Field, opened in 1924, is the oldest NFL stadium. The home of the Chicago Bears underwent extensive renovation in 2003.

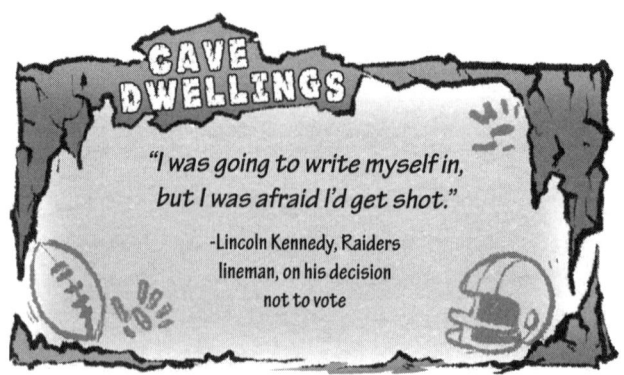

**CAVE DWELLINGS**

*"I was going to write myself in, but I was afraid I'd get shot."*

-Lincoln Kennedy, Raiders lineman, on his decision not to vote

4. A matchup of what two teams in 2015 resulted in a stunning 52-49 final score and an NFL record of 13 combined touchdown passes?

a) Panthers and Cardinals
b) Saints and Giants
c) Jaguars and Lions

5. Who are the only two teams to score at least 50 points in a Super Bowl?

a) Cowboys and 49ers
b) 49ers and Redskins
c) Bears and Seahawks

Answers: 1.A 2.B 3.C 4.B (New Orleans won.) 5.A

# Well Received

1. In 2000, who became the first player in NFL history to catch 20 passes in a single game?

a) Terrell Owens
b) Marvin Harrison
c) Antonio Freeman

2. In Super Bowl XXIII, what 49er became the first running back to ever gain over 100 receiving yards in the game?

a) Wendell Tyler
b) Earl Cooper
c) Roger Craig

3. In 2005, who became the first undrafted player in NFL history to hit the 10,000-yard receiving mark?

a) Isaac Bruce
b) Rod Smith
c) Donald Driver

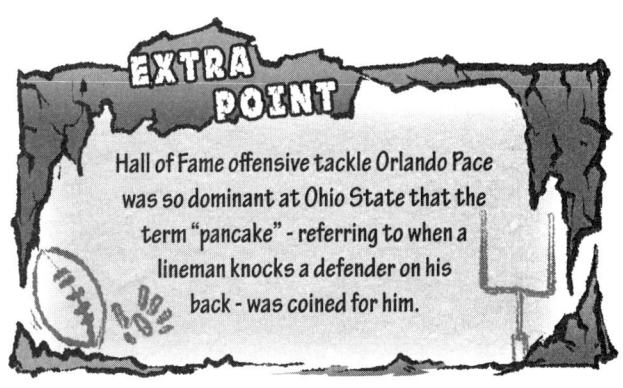

**EXTRA POINT**

Hall of Fame offensive tackle Orlando Pace was so dominant at Ohio State that the term "pancake" - referring to when a lineman knocks a defender on his back - was coined for him.

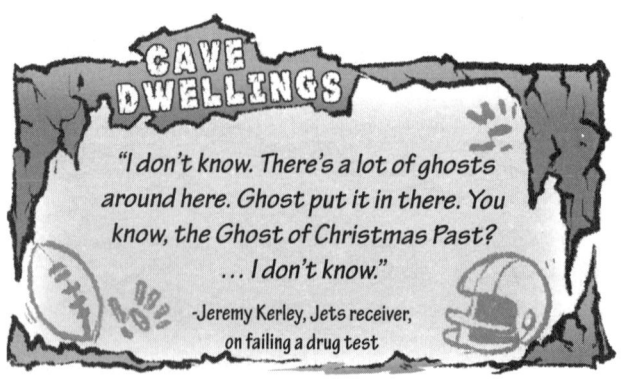

**CAVE DWELLINGS**

*"I don't know. There's a lot of ghosts around here. Ghost put it in there. You know, the Ghost of Christmas Past? ... I don't know."*

-Jeremy Kerley, Jets receiver, on failing a drug test

4. In 2011, who became the first player to lead his team in receptions and yards as an undrafted rookie since the 1970 merger?

a) Doug Baldwin
b) Victor Cruz
c) Josh Gordon

5. In 2001, what Pro Bowl receiver caught the first touchdown pass of Tom Brady's NFL career?

a) Troy Brown
b) Terry Glenn
c) Deion Branch

Answers: 1.A 2.C 3.B 4.A 5.B

# Name That Team

1. The "Flying Elvis" logo is featured on the helmet of what NFL team?

a) Patriots
b) Chiefs
c) Cardinals

2. Established in Chicago in 1898, what is the oldest continuously run pro football franchise still in operation?

a) Rams
b) Lions
c) Cardinals

3. The first team with a logo on their helmets began play in 1937 in Cleveland, where they won the NFL title in 1945 before moving the following year. Who are they?

a) Eagles
b) Rams
c) Redskins

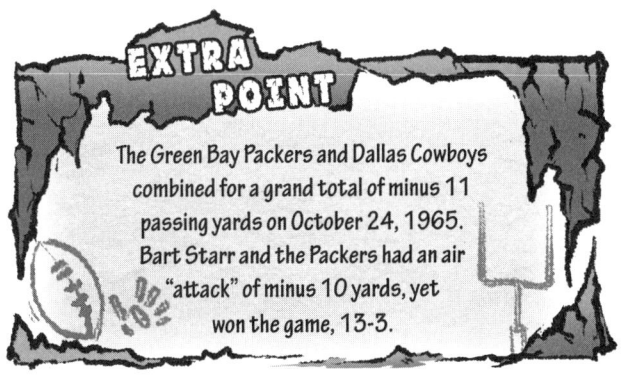

**EXTRA POINT**

The Green Bay Packers and Dallas Cowboys combined for a grand total of minus 11 passing yards on October 24, 1965. Bart Starr and the Packers had an air "attack" of minus 10 yards, yet won the game, 13-3.

**CAVE DWELLINGS**

*"Stay healthy, park in the right place, and if any teacher even mentions an exam, take it."*

-Bobby Bowden, Florida State coach, giving offseason advice to QB Chris Rix

4. Only one NFL team has won back-to-back Super Bowls with different head coaches. Who?

a) Cowboys
b) 49ers
c) Steelers

5. After spending his entire career as a Colt, Johnny Unitas played his final NFL season for this team, where he became the first QB in NFL history to pass for over 40,000 yards. Who?

a) Chargers
b) Raiders
c) Steelers

Answers: 1.A 2.C 3.B 4.B (with Bill Walsh and George Seifert) 5.A

# One for the Ages

1. At 42, who was the youngest man ever to reach 100 career victories in the NFL?

a) Norv Turner
b) Jon Gruden
c) John Madden

2. Because of his brief career, what runner was the youngest person ever inducted in the Pro Football Hall of Fame at the age of 34?

a) Barry Sanders
b) Gale Sayers
c) Terrell Davis

3. At 19, the youngest player ever drafted by an NFL team was the 10th overall pick in 2007 by the Texans. Who is he?

a) Amobi Okoye
b) Jamaal Anderson
c) Travis Johnson

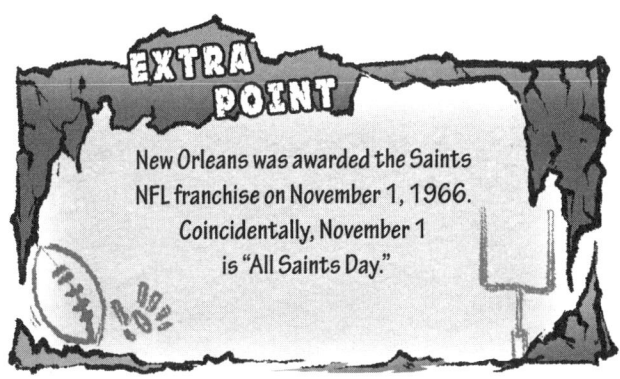

**EXTRA POINT**

New Orleans was awarded the Saints NFL franchise on November 1, 1966. Coincidentally, November 1 is "All Saints Day."

CAVE DWELLINGS

*"My mom goes about four bills."*

-Craig "Ironhead" Heyward, blaming his
300-pound frame on his mother

4. Who topped Shaun Alexander by a single yard to win the 2004 NFL rushing title as the oldest back ever to lead the league in rushing at age 31?

a) Priest Holmes
b) Tiki Barber
c) Curtis Martin

5. What 28-year-old quarterback was the winner of the 2000 Heisman Trophy?

a) Jason White
b) Chris Weinke
c) Brandon Weeden

Answers: 1.C 2.B 3.A 4.C 5.B (Florida State)

# Second Guessing

1. Bart Starr was the first player to win back-to-back Super Bowl MVP awards. Who was the second?

a) Terry Bradshaw
b) Joe Montana
c) Tom Brady

2. Eli Manning was the first quarterback selected in the 2004 NFL Draft. Who was the second one?

a) J.P. Losman
b) Philip Rivers
c) Ben Roethlisberger

3. In 2004, who became the second of only two men (after Barry Sanders) to rush for 1,000 yards in each of his first 10 NFL seasons?

a) Jerome Bettis
b) Curtis Martin
c) Emmitt Smith

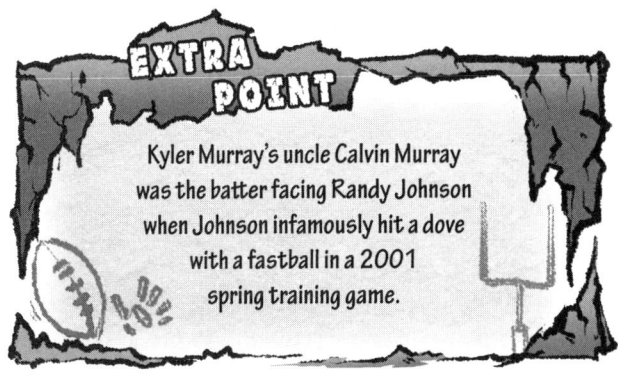

**EXTRA POINT**

Kyler Murray's uncle Calvin Murray was the batter facing Randy Johnson when Johnson infamously hit a dove with a fastball in a 2001 spring training game.

**CAVE DWELLINGS**

*"Because she's too ugly to kiss goodbye."*

-Bum Phillips, NFL coach,
on why he brought his wife
on road trips

4. Rodney Harrison was the first NFL player to record at least 30 interceptions and 30 sacks in his career. In 2010, who became the second?

a) Ray Lewis
b) Adrian Wilson
c) Brian Urlacher

5. In his 2011 induction speech, he claimed he was "the only pro football player that's in the Hall of Fame" who was "the second best player in my own family." Who said it about his brother?

a) Cris Carter
b) Bruce Matthews
c) Shannon Sharpe

Answers: 1.A 2.B 3.B 4.A 5.C (brother Sterling)

# The Name Game

1. The last pick in the NFL Draft every year is commonly referred to by what name?

a) Mr. Practice Squad
b) Mr. Pigskin
c) Mr. Irrelevant

2. What's the real first name of Pro Football Hall of Famer Crazy Legs Hirsch?

a) Elijah
b) Ethan
c) Elroy

3. What NFL franchise got its team name from a poem written by Edgar Allan Poe?

a) Baltimore Ravens
b) Carolina Panthers
c) Minnesota Vikings

EXTRA POINT

As a punter on his high school team, Warren Sapp averaged 43.5 yards a kick.

CAVE DWELLINGS

*"Leaving."*

-Jim McMahon, on his fondest
memory of BYU

4. Former Vikings Pro Bowl receiver and sportscaster Ahmad Rashad originally went by what name?

a) Joe Smith
b) Bobby Moore
c) Stephen Caruthers

5. When asked about the Dolphins defense prior to Super Bowl VI, Cowboys coach Tom Landry said he couldn't recall any specific players. This inspired what Miami moniker?

a) The No-Name Defense
b) The Anonymous Eleven
c) The Dull Fins

Answers: 1.C 2.C 3.A (*The Raven*) 4.B 5.A

# Zzzzzz

1. Of all the NFL quarterbacks whose last names begin with the letter Z, who has thrown the most touchdown passes?

a) Roy Zimmerman
b) Eric Zeier
c) Jim Zorn

2. Who is the only player whose last name begins with "Z" that is currently in the Pro Football Hall of Fame?

a) Mike Zordich
b) Gary Zimmerman
c) John Zook

3. In 2012, who became the first kicker in NFL history to hit a field goal of 50+ yards and another of 60 in the same game?

a) Carl Zander
b) Dave Zastudil
c) Greg Zuerlein

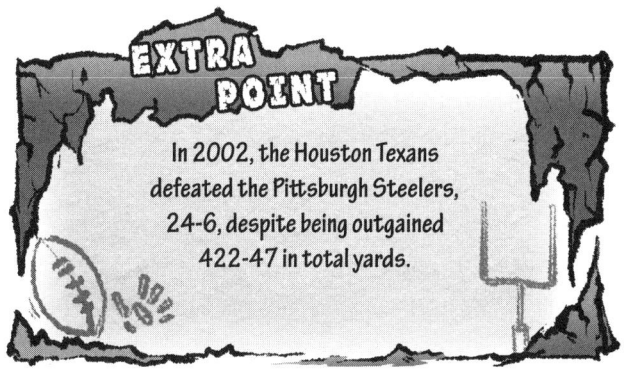

**EXTRA POINT**

In 2002, the Houston Texans defeated the Pittsburgh Steelers, 24-6, despite being outgained 422-47 in total yards.

"I do understand the allure of the maple bars."

-Pete Carroll, on his player, Golden Tate, trespassing into a donut shop at 3 a.m.

4. The Eagles shut out the Cowboys 27-0 on Thanksgiving Day 1989 in a "Bounty Bowl" contest in which Jimmy Johnson accused Buddy Ryan of placing bounties on Troy Aikman and what Dallas kicker?

a) Max Zendejas
b) Tony Zendejas
c) Luis Zendejas

5. What Raven became a pro boxer in 2006 and retired from the NFL in his late 20s in 2013?

a) Dusty Zeigler
b) Tom Zbikowski
c) Kevin Zeitler

Answers: 1.C (111) 2.B 3.C (with the Rams) 4.C 5.B

# Who Said It?

1. This Colts coach, fired after starting out 0-5 in 1991, explained, "When you see that big zero up there for wins, it's like somebody put a dead rat in your mouth."

a) Jim Mora
b) Ron Meyer
c) Frank Kush

2. When asked why his wedding was held in the morning, this "Golden Boy" said, "If it didn't work out, I didn't want to blow the whole day."

a) Paul Hornung
b) Gale Sayers
c) Earl Campbell

3. In 2008, after a 13-13 stalemate with the Bengals, he revealed, "I've never been a part of a tie. I never even knew that was in the rule book."

a) Donovan McNabb
b) Ben Roethlisberger
c) Philip Rivers

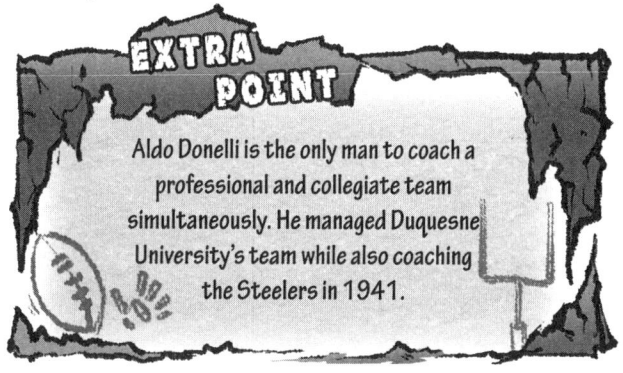

**EXTRA POINT**

Aldo Donelli is the only man to coach a professional and collegiate team simultaneously. He managed Duquesne University's team while also coaching the Steelers in 1941.

*"We're not attempting to circumcise rules."*

-Bill Cowher

4. On being the first player in over 25 years to gain 1,000 yards for a one-win team, this '90s Jets running back quizzically remarked, "I don't know if that's an honor."

a) Curtis Martin
b) Adrian Murrell
c) Blair Thomas

5. He led the league in passing yards each season from 1979-82. Years later came this proclamation: "Now that I'm retired, I want to say that all defensive linemen are sissies."

a) Ken Anderson
b) Fran Tarkenton
c) Dan Fouts

Answers: 1.B 2.A 3.A 4.B 5.C

# Goose Eggs

1. In 2009, the Patriots set a record for the largest halftime lead in NFL history, 45-0. What team wound up losing 59-0?

a) New York Jets
b) Cincinnati Bengals
c) Tennessee Titans

2. In a 2004 contest, what team was shut out for the first time since 1977 as the Seahawks put an end to their NFL record-scoring streak of 420 games?

a) New Orleans Saints
b) San Francisco 49ers
c) Minnesota Vikings

3. The Ravens held what Pro Bowler to a 0.0 QB rating in a 2004 game when he completed just 4 of 18 passes and threw two interceptions?

a) Eli Manning
b) Peyton Manning
c) Donovan McNabb

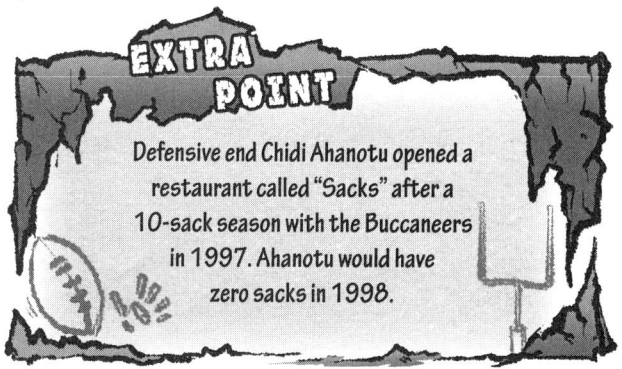

**EXTRA POINT**

Defensive end Chidi Ahanotu opened a restaurant called "Sacks" after a 10-sack season with the Buccaneers in 1997. Ahanotu would have zero sacks in 1998.

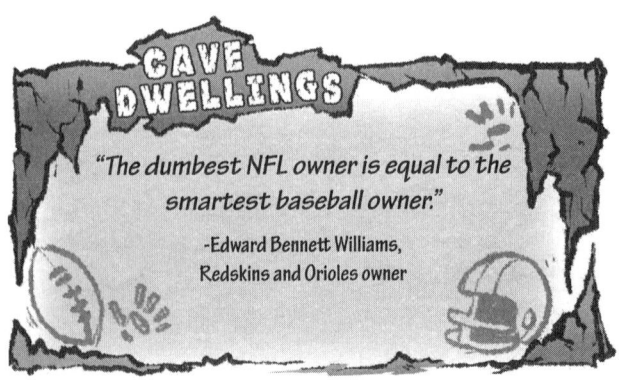

CAVE DWELLINGS

*"The dumbest NFL owner is equal to the smartest baseball owner."*

-Edward Bennett Williams,
Redskins and Orioles owner

4. The Browns were on both ends of season-opening shutout routs ten years apart against the same team – a 51-0 win in 1989 and a 43-0 loss in '99. Who did they play?

a) Miami Dolphins
b) Pittsburgh Steelers
c) San Diego Chargers

5. The last time this occurred in the NFL was way back in 1943 when the Giants played the Lions. What?

a) Each team's QB finished with 0 completions.
b) The game ended with 0 combined first downs.
c) The game ended in a 0-0 tie.

Answers: 1.C 2.B 3.A 4.B 5.C

# Where Are You?

1. The Pro Football Hall of Fame is located in Canton, Ohio, on what street?

a) Vince Lombardi Avenue
b) George Halas Drive
c) Tom Landry Lane

2. MetLife Stadium was the site for Super Bowl XLVIII, the first time the game was held in an outdoor venue in a cold weather environment. In what city was it played?

a) East Rutherford, NJ
b) Harrison, NY
c) New Brunswick, NJ

3. When the Rams moved back to Los Angeles for the 2016 season, it marked the first relocation by an NFL team since 1997, when what franchise moved to its current home?

a) Raiders
b) Cardinals
c) Titans

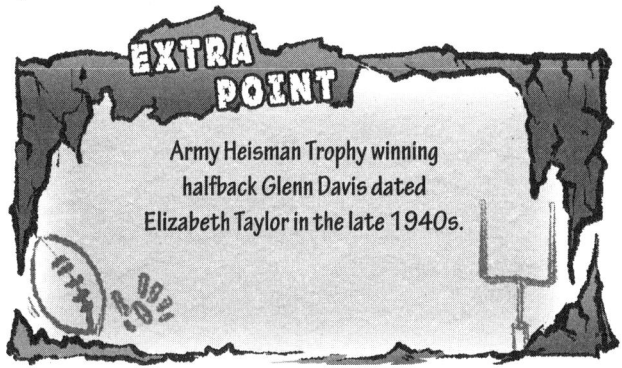

**EXTRA POINT**

Army Heisman Trophy winning halfback Glenn Davis dated Elizabeth Taylor in the late 1940s.

CAVE DWELLINGS

*"You know it was bad when the only person taking pictures in the locker room was my dad."*

-Fred Smerlas, Bills lineman, on the losing days in Buffalo

4. The 49ers Levi's Stadium is actually located nearly 40 miles from San Francisco in what California city?

a) Fresno
b) Santa Clara
c) Sacramento

5. From 2008-13, the Buffalo Bills played one "home" game a season in what Canadian city?

a) Ottawa
b) Edmonton
c) Toronto

Answers: 1.B 2.A 3.C (Then the Oilers, they moved from Houston to Tennessee.) 4.B 5.C (at the Rogers Centre)

# QB Quiz

1. What future All-Pro and fourth round pick of the Patriots in 1987 was traded to Minnesota after he balked at the idea of switching from quarterback to running back?

a) Rich Gannon
b) Trent Green
c) Jeff Garcia

2. With 27, what player holds the NFL mark for the most touchdown passes thrown by a rookie quarterback?

a) Baker Mayfield
b) Andrew Luck
c) Joe Flacco

3. What Hall of Fame quarterback was drafted by the Steelers in 1955 but cut before the season even began?

a) Y.A. Tittle
b) Bart Starr
c) Johnny Unitas

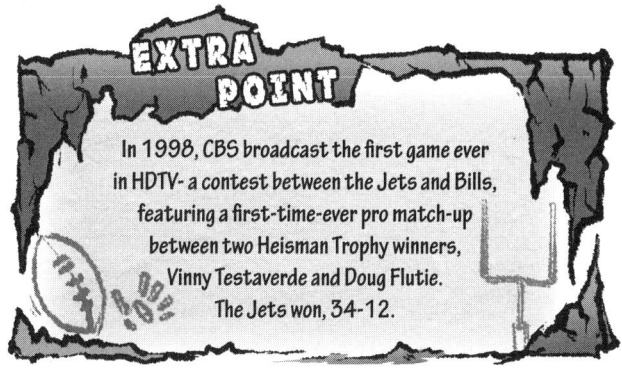

**EXTRA POINT**

In 1998, CBS broadcast the first game ever in HDTV- a contest between the Jets and Bills, featuring a first-time-ever pro match-up between two Heisman Trophy winners, Vinny Testaverde and Doug Flutie. The Jets won, 34-12.

**CAVE DWELLINGS**

*"Every time I look up, it seems we're punting."*

-John McKay, Buccaneers coach, during the early years of the Tampa Bay franchise

4. While no other player has done it more than once, what quarterback has thrown for over 5,000 yards in a season five times in his career?

a) Matthew Stafford
b) Aaron Rodgers
c) Drew Brees

5. In the 2003 NFL Playoffs, what Cowboy became the only quarterback to start a postseason game between the Aikman and Romo eras?

a) Drew Bledsoe
b) Quincy Carter
c) Jason Garrett

Answers: 1.A 2.A 3.C 4.C 5.B

# Screen Test

1. *Brian's Song* was a television movie about a Chicago Bears running back. What was Brian's last name?

a) Piccolo
b) Cranston
c) Murphy

2. What quarterback teamed up with Jim Carrey in the 1994 film *Ace Ventura: Pet Detective*?

a) Terry Bradshaw
b) Troy Aikman
c) Dan Marino

3. In the 1993 movie *Rudy*, Sean Astin stars as Rudy Ruettiger, a small football player who overcomes the odds to play in a college game for what team?

a) USC
b) Notre Dame
c) Michigan

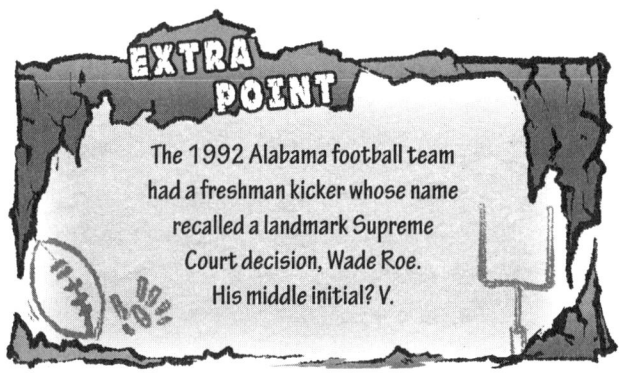

**EXTRA POINT**

The 1992 Alabama football team had a freshman kicker whose name recalled a landmark Supreme Court decision, Wade Roe. His middle initial? V.

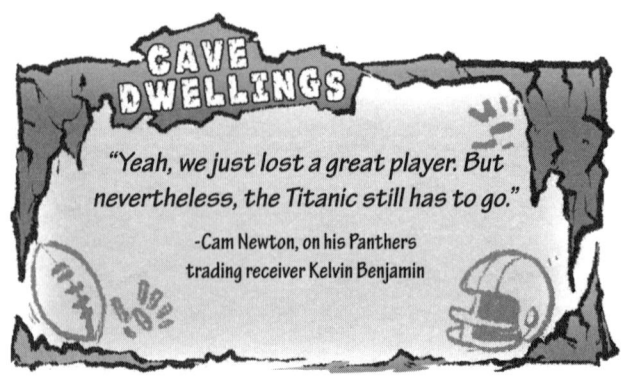

"Yeah, we just lost a great player. But nevertheless, the Titanic still has to go."

-Cam Newton, on his Panthers
trading receiver Kelvin Benjamin

4. The 2014 movie *Draft Day* focuses on the fictionalized general manager and war room actions of what NFL team?

a) New York Jets
b) Cleveland Browns
c) Buffalo Bills

5. What Pro Football Hall of Famer starred in the 1967 war film *The Dirty Dozen?*

a) Merlin Olsen
b) Jim Brown
c) Alex Karras

Answers: 1.A 2.C 3.B 4.B 5.B

# It's Official

1. When the Giants played the Patriots in Super Bowl XLII, who became the first black referee to be chosen as the head official in a Super Bowl?

a) Jerome Boger
b) Mike Carey
c) Walt Anderson

2. When you see a flag on the play, it's a yellow one. What color were NFL officials' flags until the mid-1960s?

a) Red
b) White
c) Blue

3. In 2004, the excessive jamming of receivers by cornerbacks led the NFL to place more emphasis on a rule first named after what Steelers Hall of Famer?

a) Mel Blount
b) Jack Butler
c) Jack Ham

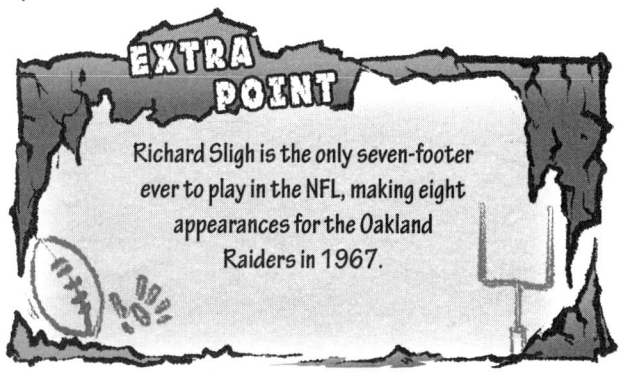

**EXTRA POINT**

Richard Sligh is the only seven-footer ever to play in the NFL, making eight appearances for the Oakland Raiders in 1967.

*"Do we have to start at one?"*

-Tom Landry, when asked to rate his
team's secondary on a scale of one to ten

4. In the 2001 Playoffs, referee Walt Coleman overturned Tom Brady's game-changing fumble against the Raiders by citing what obscure rule?

a) Glove rule
b) Intention rule
c) Tuck rule

5. In a contest officiated by replacement refs, who came down with the winning touchdown in the 2012 "Fail Mary" game in which Seattle beat Green Bay on the controversial final play?

a) Zach Miller
b) Golden Tate
c) Sidney Rice

Answers: 1.B 2.B 3.A 4.C 5.B

# Secondary Squads

1. While his only season with them was the final one of his career, Franco Harris became the first player from what team to be inducted into the Pro Football Hall of Fame in 1990?

a) Tampa Bay Buccaneers
b) Seattle Seahawks
c) New Orleans Saints

2. With what team did Steve Young begin his NFL career before being dealt to the 49ers in 1987?

a) Tampa Bay Buccaneers
b) Philadelphia Eagles
c) Miami Dolphins

3. On what team did Jerry Rice catch his final touchdown in the NFL?

a) Oakland Raiders
b) Denver Broncos
c) Seattle Seahawks

**EXTRA POINT**

Halfback Fred Gehrke, a sideline artist, painted horns on the Rams helmets in 1948. That's been the team's logo ever since.

*"This is something that probably doesn't happen in Tom Landry's office."*

-Sam Wyche, Bengals coach, on the team cat vomiting in his office

4. Before he became a multiple All-Pro as a Chief, Priest Holmes was the first 1,000-yard rusher in the history of what team in the 1990s?

a) Jacksonville Jaguars
b) Carolina Panthers
c) Baltimore Ravens

5. Joe Montana and Marcus Allen became legends with other NFL teams before playing together on what squad in 1993 and '94?

a) Buffalo Bills
b) Kansas City Chiefs
c) Chicago Bears

Answers: 1.B 2.A 3.C 4.C 5.B

# The AFL

1. What 1964 American Football League MVP who played from 1960-70 is the all-time leading scorer in the league's history?

a) George Blanda
b) Abner Haynes
c) Gino Cappelletti

2. "Bambi" was the first AFL star selected to the Pro Football Hall of Fame. Who is he?

a) George Blanda
b) Lance Alworth
c) Clem Daniels

3. Who is the only player to rush for 1,000 yards in a single season in both the AFL and NFL?

a) Mike Garrett
b) Floyd Little
c) O.J. Simpson

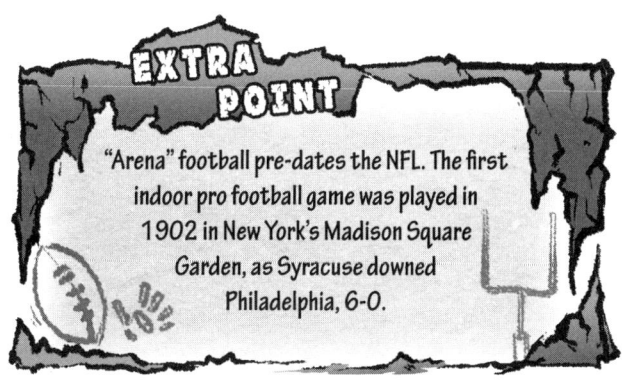

**EXTRA POINT**

"Arena" football pre-dates the NFL. The first indoor pro football game was played in 1902 in New York's Madison Square Garden, as Syracuse downed Philadelphia, 6-0.

CAVE DWELLINGS

*"We were so poor a robber once broke into our house and we ended up robbing the robber."*

-Shannon Sharpe

4. Who passed for more yards than anyone else in the history of the AFL?

a) Len Dawson
b) Jack Kemp
c) Joe Namath

5. With three, what franchise won more American Football League championships than any other?

a) New York Jets
b) Boston Patriots
c) Dallas Texans/Kansas City Chiefs

Answers: 1.C 2.B 3.A 4.B (21,130 yards) 5.C

# Prized Possessions

1. The Heisman Trophy is named in honor of the former athletic director of the Downtown Athletic Club, the award's originator. What is Heisman's first name?

a) Paul
b) John
c) Ringo

2. What trophy is given to the champion of the Canadian Football League?

a) Grey Cup
b) Canadian Cup
c) Calder Cup

3. Which two college football teams vie for the Little Brown Jug?

a) Penn State and Michigan State
b) Indiana and Purdue
c) Michigan and Minnesota

**EXTRA POINT**

Sam Darnold's grandfather, Dick Hammer, was the Marlboro Man during the 1970s.

**CAVE DWELLINGS**

*"I played four years in Detroit. I can handle (getting hit by) a car."*

-Joey Harrington, after being seriously injured when the bike he was riding was struck by an SUV

4. What award does the Super Bowl MVP receive?

a) Pete Rozelle Trophy
b) George Halas Trophy
c) Lamar Hunt Trophy

5. The NFL's Man of the Year Award is named after what football legend?

a) Deacon Jones
b) Walter Payton
c) Johnny Unitas

Answers: 1.B 2.A 3.C 4.A 5.B

# Holiday Hits

1. In the longest game in NFL history, the Chiefs lost a double overtime playoff contest to what squad on Christmas Day, 1971?

a) Oakland Raiders
b) New York Jets
c) Miami Dolphins

2. In a Raiders-Colts playoff game on December 24, 1977, what QB, born on Christmas, 1945, hit Dave Casper for the winning score in a double-overtime classic?

a) Ken Stabler
b) Bert Jones
c) Tom Flores

3. On the night before Christmas and then New Years Eve, 1983, what team handed John Elway and Dan Marino their first playoff defeats?

a) Houston Oilers
b) Buffalo Bills
c) Seattle Seahawks

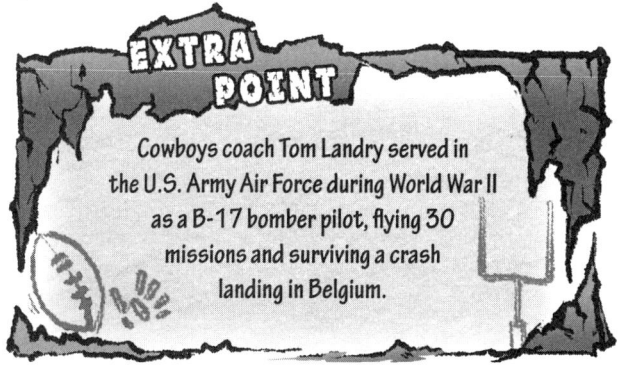

### EXTRA POINT

Cowboys coach Tom Landry served in the U.S. Army Air Force during World War II as a B-17 bomber pilot, flying 30 missions and surviving a crash landing in Belgium.

*"They don't like my overhand delivery."*

-Bubba Smith, All-Pro defensive end,
on being banned from bowling alleys

4. During their 2000 title run, Brian Billick had his Ravens use a different word when discussing "playoffs." It's the December 23rd holiday that *Seinfeld* made famous. What?

a) Kwannnukah
b) Festivus
c) Merry Day

5. Born in Santa Claus, Indiana, what "giving" quarterback led the NFL in interceptions in 2009 and was sacked the most times the following season?

a) Jay Cutler
b) Eli Manning
c) Brett Favre

Answers: 1.C 2.A 3.C 4.B 5.A

# Who's In Charge Here?

1. For what NFL team did former 49ers hero Dwight Clark serve as the general manager from the late 1990s to the early 2000s?

a) Denver Broncos
b) Cleveland Browns
c) Dallas Cowboys

2. What Eagles founder was instrumental in instituting the NFL Draft and later served as the league's commissioner?

a) Pete Rozelle
b) Joseph Carr
c) Bert Bell

3. What Baltimore Colts receiver went on to become the founder and majority owner of the Carolina Panthers over three decades later?

a) Jerry Richardson
b) Raymond Berry
c) Jimmy Orr

**EXTRA POINT**

Before 1948, NFL officials blew horns to signal penalties.

"When you're rich, you don't write checks...Straight cash, homey."

-Randy Moss, on how he intended to pay a $10,000 fine

4. In 1972, owners Carroll Rosenbloom and Robert Irsay pulled off a rare move when they swapped NFL franchises. Rosenbloom's Colts went to Irsay in exchange for what team?

a) Oakland Raiders
b) Los Angeles Rams
c) St. Louis Cardinals

5. What future Hall of Famer became the first President of the NFL Players Association in 1970?

a) John Hannah
b) Franco Harris
c) John Mackey

Answers: 1.B 2.C 3.A 4.B 5.C

# Six-Point Celebrations

1. What Packer was credited with making the first-ever "Lambeau Leap" in 1993?

a) Sterling Sharpe
b) LeRoy Butler
c) Reggie White

2. In 2000, Cowboy George Teague was ejected after shoving what Pro Bowl receiver off the Dallas midfield star logo when he tried to celebrate after scoring a touchdown?

a) Randy Moss
b) Chad Johnson
c) Terrell Owens

3. After scoring in a game at Cleveland in 2007, what colorful receiver made good on his promise by leaping into the Dawg Pound?

a) Randy Moss
b) Chad Johnson
c) Terrell Owens

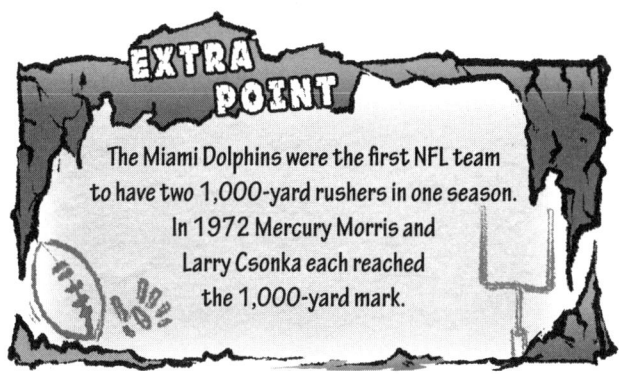

**EXTRA POINT**

The Miami Dolphins were the first NFL team to have two 1,000-yard rushers in one season. In 1972 Mercury Morris and Larry Csonka each reached the 1,000-yard mark.

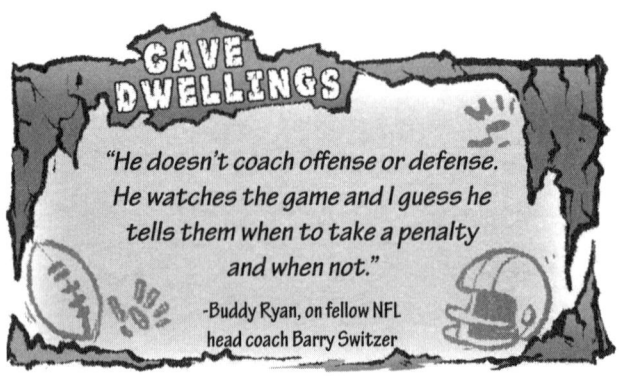

## CAVE DWELLINGS

*"He doesn't coach offense or defense. He watches the game and I guess he tells them when to take a penalty and when not."*

-Buddy Ryan, on fellow NFL head coach Barry Switzer

4. He became the first-known player to perform a touchdown dance at the University of Houston. He carried his moves with him into the NFL with the Chiefs in the 1970s. He is...?

a) Elmo Wright
b) Ed Podolak
c) Otis Taylor

5. What NFL team popularized their "Dirty Bird" touchdown celebration in the late 1990s?

a) Atlanta Falcons
b) Seattle Seahawks
c) Philadelphia Eagles

Answers: 1.B 2.C 3.B 4.A 5.A

# The Blooper Reel

1. In a 1964 game as a Viking, who provided a blooper reel fixture when he recovered a fumble and returned it 66 yards in the wrong direction to hand the 49ers a safety?

a) Jim Marshall
b) Carl Eller
c) Alan Page

2. What Cowboy infamously botched the hold on what should have been a 19-yard game-winning field goal try in the 2006 playoffs vs. Seattle?

a) Drew Bledsoe
b) Tony Romo
c) Vinny Testaverde

3. Brett Favre's very first pass as a Packer was certainly one to remember. What happened?

a) His pass hit his own lineman before being intercepted.
b) He caught his own deflected pass.
c) He hit a referee in the head.

**EXTRA POINT**

The Pittsburgh Steelers had just one losing season at home in their 30 years at Three Rivers Stadium.

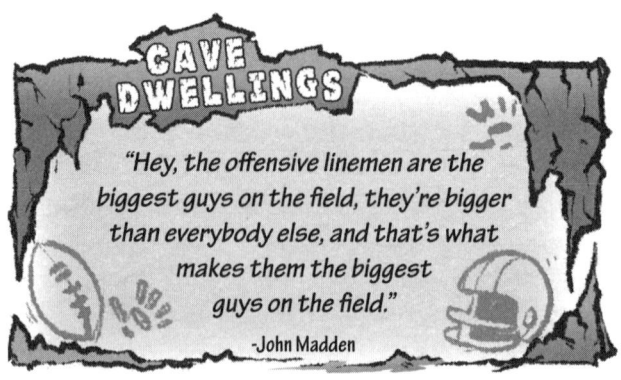

**CAVE DWELLINGS**

*"Hey, the offensive linemen are the biggest guys on the field, they're bigger than everybody else, and that's what makes them the biggest guys on the field."*

-John Madden

4. Against the Bears in the 1985 Playoffs, what Giant whiffed on a punt near his own end zone, handing Chicago six points and contributing to New York's 21-0 loss?

a) Sean Landeta
b) Dave Jennings
c) Jeff Hostetler

5. In Super Bowl XXVII, this showboating Cowboy, nearing the end zone on a fumble recovery, was caught from behind just shy of the goal line and lost the ball for a Buffalo touchback. Who is he?

a) Darren Woodson
b) Ken Norton
c) Leon Lett

# The Injured List

1. What safety was involved in the injuries that ended seasons for both Tom Brady (2008) and Wes Welker (2009)?

a) Ed Reed
b) Abram Elam
c) Bernard Pollard

2. With rookie Troy Aikman injured, who was the starting quarterback in the Cowboys only win during the 1989 season?

a) Steve Walsh
b) Tony Eason
c) Gary Hogeboom

3. Who signed with the Browns to become the highest-paid center in NFL history in 2006 before having to retire due to a serious knee injury?

a) Dominic Raiola
b) LeCharles Bentley
c) Kevin Shaffer

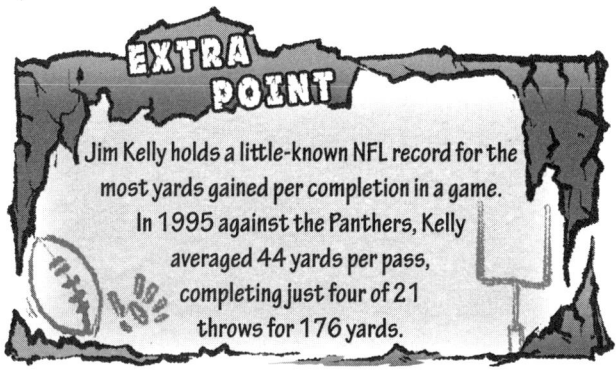

**EXTRA POINT**

Jim Kelly holds a little-known NFL record for the most yards gained per completion in a game. In 1995 against the Panthers, Kelly averaged 44 yards per pass, completing just four of 21 throws for 176 yards.

CAVE DWELLINGS

*"I didn't know big guys had groins. I'm finding out today that I actually have one."*

-Norman Hand, defensive tackle, on straining his groin

4. In 2012, what Kansas City lineman went on a postgame tirade about Chiefs fans who cheered when teammate Matt Cassel suffered an injury late in the game and lay on the ground?

a) Eric Fisher
b) Branden Albert
c) Eric Winston

5. After a solid rookie year with New England, what runner blew out his knee in a beach flag football game and never returned to the Pats?

a) Robert Edwards
b) Cecil Collins
c) Marion Butts

Answers: 1.C 2.A 3.B 4.C 5.A

# What's What?

1. What was unusual about the second half kickoff in the first Super Bowl?

a) It never happened.
b) The Packers kicked off twice.
c) A fan ran onto the field and tried to tackle the returner.

2. From 1965-81, the Dallas Cowboys set a league record that still stands for doing what 17 consecutive times?

a) Winning their season opener
b) Losing their season finale
c) Winning back-to-back games to close out the regular season

3. Fred Dryer is the only player to have done this twice in a single NFL game. What?

a) Miss an extra point
b) Return a blocked field goal for a touchdown
c) Record a safety

**EXTRA POINT**

The Steelers made Notre Dame quarterback William Shakespeare their first pick in the 1936 NFL Draft.

**CAVE DWELLINGS**

*"Any kid who would leave that wonderful weather is too dumb to play for us."*

-Alex Agase, Purdue football coach, on not recruiting in California

4. In 1992, the Bills beat the 49ers 34-31. What NFL first did both teams combine for when all was said and done?

a) Steve Young and Jim Kelly each threw for 500 yards.
b) Not a single penalty was called.
c) Neither team punted once in the entire game.

5. The 1983 Packers set a new NFL record by doing what five times in the regular season?

a) Playing an overtime game
b) Losing a game by at least 30 points
c) Having two players each rush for 100 yards in a game

Answers: 1.B (Because NBC missed it, officials asked the Packers to kick off again so it could be aired.) 2.A 3.C 4.C 5.A

# The Super Bowl

"If it's the ultimate
game, how come they're
playing it again
next year?"

-Duane Thomas

# SB QBs

1. Who was the first player in NFL history to start at quarterback in the Super Bowl for two different teams?

a) Trent Dilfer
b) Fran Tarkenton
c) Craig Morton

2. What New England quarterback became the first starter in Super Bowl history to fail to complete a pass?

a) Drew Bledsoe
b) Steve Grogan
c) Tony Eason

3. Dallas' Larry Brown was the MVP of Super Bowl XXX. Ironically, the Steelers QB he picked off twice was once the NFL's career leader in interception percentage. Who?

a) Jim Kelly
b) Neil O'Donnell
c) Kordell Stewart

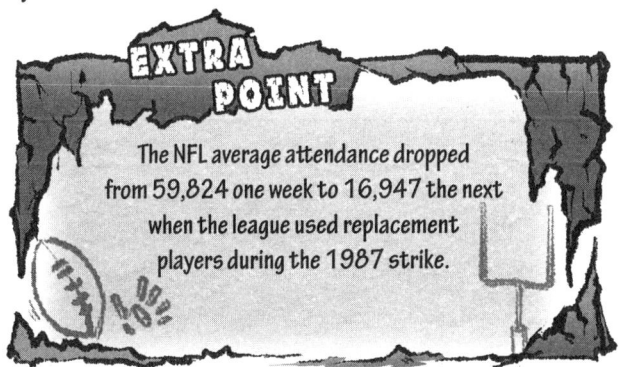

**EXTRA POINT**

The NFL average attendance dropped from 59,824 one week to 16,947 the next when the league used replacement players during the 1987 strike.

### CAVE DWELLINGS

*"Probably The Beatles' White Album."*

-Steve Largent, on which one of his
records he cherished the most

4. Who became the first left-handed quarterback to win a Super Bowl (XI) when his Raiders defeated the Vikings?

a) Ken Stabler
b) Daryle Lamonica
c) Tom Flores

5. What two Super Bowl-winning quarterbacks share the NFL record for touchdowns without an interception in an entire postseason, with 11?

a) Tom Brady and Peyton Manning
b) Joe Flacco and Joe Montana
c) Kurt Warner and Drew Brees

Answers: 1.C (with the Cowboys and Broncos) 2.C (Super Bowl XX) 3.B 4.A 5.B

# Stadia-Mania

1. What Florida venue hosted three of the first five Super Bowls?

a) Joe Robbie Stadium
b) Tampa Stadium
c) The Orange Bowl

2. Super Bowl VIII between Minnesota and Miami was the first to be played at a venue that wasn't the home of a current NFL team. What Texas facility hosted it?

a) War Memorial Stadium
b) Cotton Bowl
c) Rice Stadium

3. Super Bowl XXX between the Steelers and Cowboys would be the last to be held on a college campus. Where was it?

a) Autzen Stadium (Oregon)
b) Sun Devil Stadium (Arizona)
c) Stanford Stadium (California)

**EXTRA POINT**

James Eggink was one of the Montreal Alouettes choices in the 1996 CFL Draft. The problem? He died in December 1995.

**CAVE DWELLINGS**

*"You take a gun and shoot him before the game."*

-Jim Haslett, NFL player and coach,
on how to handle Hall of Fame
guard John Hannah

4. The Cowboys beat the Broncos in the first-ever indoor Super Bowl (XII), played in a city that has hosted double-digit Super Bowls. What's the venue?

a) New Orleans Superdome
b) Minneapolis Metrodome
c) Pontiac Silverdome

5. With a crowd of only two-thirds capacity, what venue hosted the first Super Bowl?

a) Tulane Stadium
b) Los Angeles Memorial Coliseum
c) Rose Bowl

Answers: 1.C 2.C 3.B (on the campus of Arizona State University) 4.A 5.B

# MVP!

1. Who is the only quarterback to be named Super Bowl MVP without throwing a touchdown in the game?

a) Joe Namath
b) Bob Griese
c) Jim Plunkett

2. Two players have been named the NFL's Defensive Player of the Year and Super Bowl MVP in the same season. Who are they?

a) Chuck Howley and Richard Dent
b) Ray Lewis and Lawrence Taylor
c) Harvey Martin and Ray Lewis

3. In Super Bowl XXXI, who became the first special teams player ever to be named the game's MVP?

a) Troy Brown
b) Dexter Jackson
c) Desmond Howard

**EXTRA POINT**

The University of Florida Gators accidentally published a crocodile on their media guide cover in 2003.

CAVE DWELLINGS

*"I'd like to thank my hands for being so great."*

—Freddie Mitchell, after an Eagles win in which he converted the famous "4th and 26" vs. the Packers in the 2003 NFL Playoffs

4. What MVP of Super Bowl XI remains the only receiver to win the award with under 100 yards receiving?

a) John Stallworth
b) Fred Biletnikoff
c) Bob Hayes

5. After Super Bowl XXI, what QB became the first Super Bowl MVP to utter the now-famous phrase "I'm going to Disney World" on TV?

a) Phil Simms
b) Joe Montana
c) Troy Aikman

Answers: 1.A (Super Bowl III) 2.C (Martin was the co-MVP of SB XII.) 3.C (with the Packers) 4.B (Raiders) 5.A

# Streaking

1. What backup quarterback of the Bills and Chargers was a member of five consecutive losing Super Bowl teams in the 1990s?

a) Gale Gilbert
b) Frank Reich
c) Stan Humphries

2. With two sacks and a forced fumble in Super Bowl XLIII against Arizona, what Steeler established a new postseason record with four straight multi-sack games?

a) James Farrior
b) Lamarr Woodley
c) James Harrison

3. What team failed to scored a single first half touchdown in each of its first four Super Bowl appearances?

a) Minnesota Vikings
b) Buffalo Bills
c) Miami Dolphins

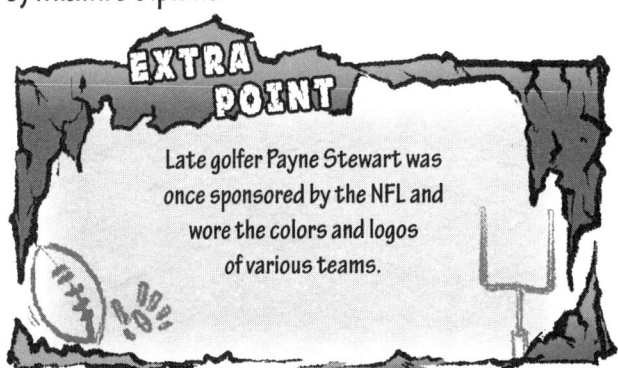

**EXTRA POINT**

Late golfer Payne Stewart was once sponsored by the NFL and wore the colors and logos of various teams.

*"I've been big ever since I was little."*

-William "Refrigerator" Perry

4. En route to his second MVP, what quarterback set a new record by beginning Super Bowl XLVI with nine consecutive completions?

a) Eli Manning
b) Tom Brady
c) Ben Roethlisberger

5. What team ran off 24 consecutive points en route to claiming its second straight Super Bowl title in 1974?

a) Pittsburgh Steelers
b) Dallas Cowboys
c) Miami Dolphins

Answers: 1.A 2.B 3.A 4.A 5.C (SB VIII over the Vikings)

# Unlikely Heroes

1. What Patriot, who scored the winning TD of Super Bowl LI, set Super Bowl records with 14 receptions and 20 points scored (three touchdowns and a two-point conversion)?

a) James White
b) Dion Lewis
c) Malcolm Mitchell

2. With just three interceptions on the season, what defensive back recorded two in Super Bowl XXXVII and was named the game's MVP?

a) Larry Brown
b) Dwight Smith
c) Dexter Jackson

3. In Super Bowl XXII, what little-known runner became the first player in the game's history to surpass 200 yards rushing?

a) Clarence Harmon
b) Tommie Agee
c) Timmy Smith

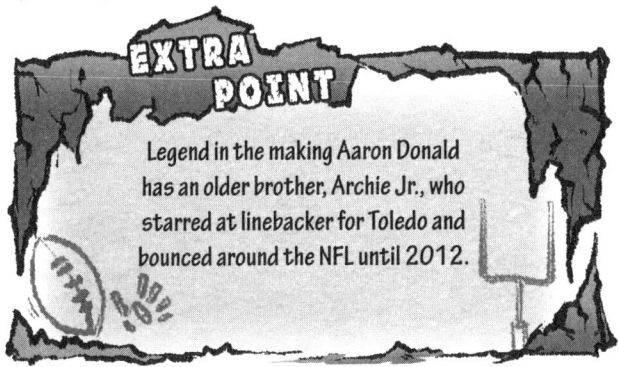

**EXTRA POINT**

Legend in the making Aaron Donald has an older brother, Archie Jr., who starred at linebacker for Toledo and bounced around the NFL until 2012.

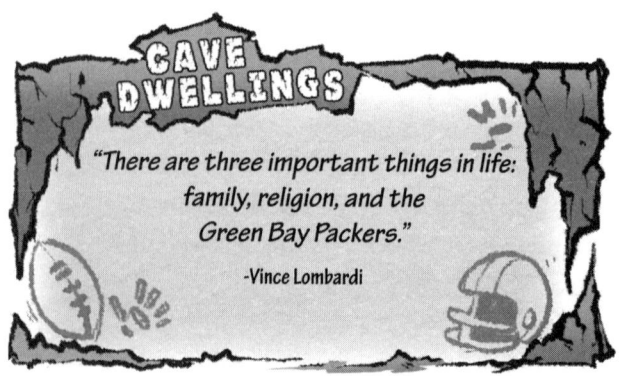

**CAVE DWELLINGS**

*"There are three important things in life: family, religion, and the Green Bay Packers."*

-Vince Lombardi

4. In their near-upset of the Steelers in Super Bowl XLIII, what Cardinal nearly matched his season total when he tied Reggie White's record with three sacks in the game?

a) Darnell Dockett
b) Calvin Pace
c) Karlos Dansby

5. What Broncos back had just three rushing TDs in his entire NFL career before scoring two in Denver's win over Atlanta in Super Bowl XXXIII?

a) Howard Griffith
b) Derek Loville
c) Detron Smith

Answers: 1.A 2.C (Buccaneers) 3.C (Redskins) 4.A 5.A

# First Class to Coach

1. What starter on Chicago's Super Bowl XX team earned a second ring as the Colts defensive backs coach in their win over the Bears in Super Bowl XLI?

a) Doug Plank
b) Mike Singletary
c) Leslie Frazier

2. What Colts Hall of Famer coached the New England Patriots to their first Super Bowl appearance (XX) in 1986?

a) Raymond Berry
b) Ron Meyer
c) Jim Parker

3. Who was the first man ever to win a Super Bowl ring as a player and a head coach?

a) Sean Payton
b) Don McCafferty
c) Tom Flores

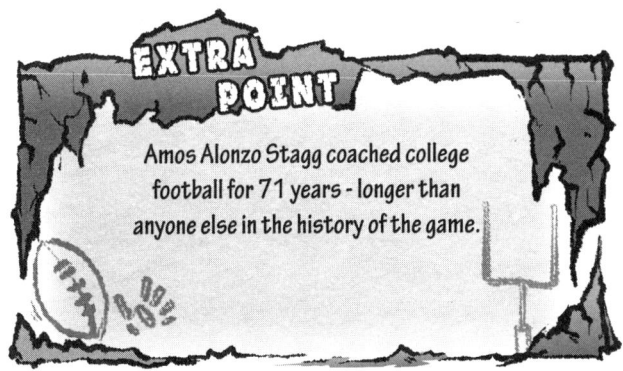

**EXTRA POINT**

Amos Alonzo Stagg coached college football for 71 years - longer than anyone else in the history of the game.

"The money, first and foremost."

-Chester Taylor, on why he
signed with the Bears

4. What Super Bowl MVP went on to become an NFL head coach for the team he played for?

a) Jake Scott
b) Bart Starr
c) Len Dawson

5. Tony Dungy won a Super Bowl as both a player and a coach. His first ring came after Super Bowl XIII as a defensive back with what team?

a) Pittsburgh Steelers
b) Dallas Cowboys
c) Miami Dolphins

Answers: 1.C 2.A 3.C (with the Chiefs and Raiders, respectively) 4.B (Packers) 5.A

# Exclusive Excellence

1. Who is the only coach to lead one team to three Super Bowl wins with three different starting quarterbacks?

a) Joe Gibbs
b) Bill Cowher
c) Bill Parcells

2. In their loss to the Steelers, the longest play in Super Bowl X for the Cowboys was a 34-yard TD pass from Roger Staubach to this man- the only reception of his NFL career. Who is he?

a) Calvin Hill
b) Golden Richards
c) Percy Howard

3. Who is the only player to have three rushing touchdowns in one Super Bowl?

a) Emmitt Smith
b) Curtis Martin
c) Terrell Davis

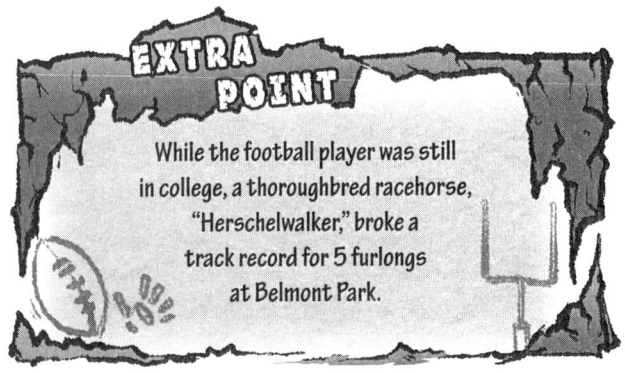

**EXTRA POINT**

While the football player was still in college, a thoroughbred racehorse, "Herschelwalker," broke a track record for 5 furlongs at Belmont Park.

**CAVE DWELLINGS**

*"Think I'm not biased tonight? Well, I am."*

-Don Meredith, on *Monday Night Football*, as his former Cowboys team took on the Rams

4. When this former Colt beat Baltimore in Super Bowl III as a Jet, he became the only player ever to win an NFL, AFL and Super Bowl championship. He is…?

a) Johnny Sample
b) Matt Snell
c) Babe Parilli

5. What is the only team to win back-to-back Super Bowls on more than one occasion?

a) Pittsburgh Steelers
b) San Francisco 49ers
c) New England Patriots

Answers: 1.A (Redskins) 2.C 3.C (SB XXXII) 4.A 5.A

# The End

1. Jerome Bettis went out in style, ending his playing career with a Super Bowl XL Steelers win in his hometown. Where was the game played?

a) Detroit's Ford Field
b) Miami's Dolphin Stadium
c) San Diego's Qualcomm Stadium

2. John Elway's NFL career came to an end after Denver's Super Bowl win over what team?

a) Green Bay Packers
b) Atlanta Falcons
c) Washington Redskins

3. In his final NFL game, what Packer kicked four field goals in their Super Bowl II win over the Raiders?

a) Randy Walker
b) Paul Hornung
c) Don Chandler

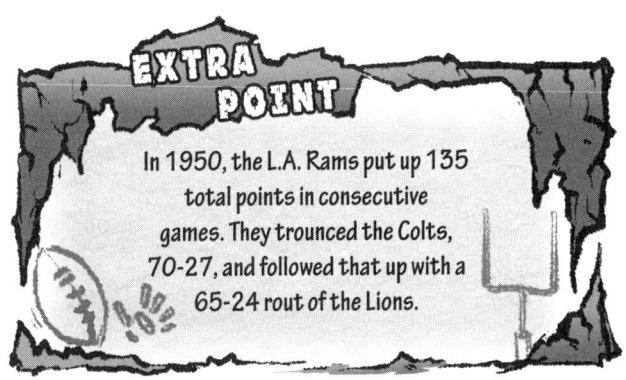

**EXTRA POINT**

In 1950, the L.A. Rams put up 135 total points in consecutive games. They trounced the Colts, 70-27, and followed that up with a 65-24 rout of the Lions.

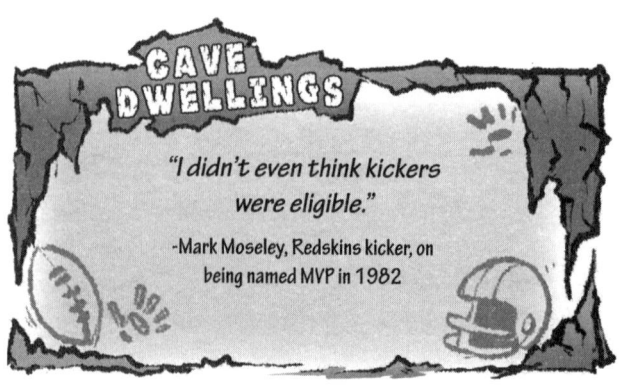

**CAVE DWELLINGS**

*"I didn't even think kickers were eligible."*

-Mark Moseley, Redskins kicker, on being named MVP in 1982

4. What Titan came up a yard short against the Rams in Super Bowl XXXIV, failing to reach the end zone as time ran out and leaving Tennessee with a heartbreaking 23-16 defeat?

a) Kevin Dyson
b) Frank Wycheck
c) Derrick Mason

5. The final game this Raiders Hall of Fame linebacker ever played came in a 38-9 Super Bowl XVIII drubbing of the Redskins. Who is he?

a) Ted Hendricks
b) Howie Long
c) Gene Upshaw

Answers: 1.A 2.B (SB XXXIII) 3.C 4.A 5.A

# Postgame Chatter

*"Look- It's the National*
*Football League.*
*Nobody died."*

-Bill Belichick, on how he handled
a shocking last-second defeat
to the Dolphins in 2018

"Well, we didn't block real good, but we made up for it by not tackling."
*–John McKay, Buccaneers coach*

"We can't run. We can't pass. We can't stop the run. We can't stop the pass. We can't kick. Other than that, we're just not a very good football team right now."
*–Bruce Coslet, Bengals coach*

"In my opinion, if we are going to have a good season, we have to put together more back-to-back wins."
*–Jim Fassel, Giants coach*

"Our strength is that we don't have any weaknesses. Our weakness is that we don't have any real strengths."
*–Frank Broyles, Missouri and Arkansas football coach*

"Concentration-wise, we're having trouble crossing the line mentally from a toughness standpoint."
*–Bill Parcells*

"We were tipping off our plays. Whenever we broke from the huddle, three backs were laughing and one was pale as a ghost."
*–John Breen, Oilers GM, on a poor Houston team*

"I feel like I'm playing against two teams –our offense and their offense."
–Cris Dishman, Oilers cornerback, on his squad


"We just have to take our belt and tighten it another notch. I think I'm down to an 18-inch waist."
–George McIntyre, Vanderbilt coach, on losing his seventh starter to injury early in the season


"There is absolutely no truth to the rumor that the Browns highlight film will be a Polaroid shot."
–Art Modell, Browns owner, after his team's losing season


"It's hard to believe, but the score started at 0-0."
–Dennis Green, Northwestern coach, on losing a game 64-0


"I don't even go to self-service gasoline stations anymore because I don't want to have to walk in and pay for it."
–Sam Wyche, Bengals coach, on his team's 0-5 start


"Well, we've determined that we can't win at home and we can't win on the road. What we need is a neutral site."
–John McKay, Buccaneers coach, on his 0-14 Tampa Bay squad

"I called up Dial-A-Prayer and they hung up on me."
–*Mack Brown, Tulane coach, after his team lost its first seven games*

"Wehrli's become one of my best receivers."
–*Roger Staubach, after Cardinals defensive back Roger Wehrli intercepted three of his passes*

"How much powdered sugar do you want me to put on dog s*** to make it taste good? We're 0-5."
–*Gary Plummer, 49ers linebacker, on what he told team executives who scolded him for being critical of the team on radio broadcasts*

"I don't know how I feel. I'll have to go kiss my sister and see which is better."
–*Scott Campbell, Purdue quarterback, after a 29-29 tie*

"Sometimes I feel like I'm on the aft deck of the Lusitania."
–*Bob Moore, Buccaneers tight end, on his team losing every game*

"It wasn't blowing my blouse up out there, I'll tell you that."
–*Andy Reid, on his Eagles Wildcat offense generating seven yards on six plays*

"Until we win more than we lose, we're going to be losers."
–*Romeo Crennel, Browns coach*

"We've got to find a way to win. I'm willing to start cheating."
–*Marv Cook, Patriots tight end*

"You're not going to win every game, but I hate to prove it right off the bat."
–*Jerry Burns, after losing his debut as Vikings coach*

"Yeah- how to tackle."
–*Cliff Stoudt, Steelers quarterback, when asked if he learned anything after a multi-interception game*

"The only way I know to cut down on our fumbles is to punt on first down every series. Even then, we might fumble the snap."
–*Barry Switzer, on his struggling Oklahoma team*

"If didn't enjoy gloating so much, I probably wouldn't do as many interviews."
–*Jimmy Johnson*

"It's not whether you win or lose, but who gets the blame."
–*Blaine Nye, Cowboys guard*

"If you can't make the putts and can't get the man in from second in the bottom of the ninth, you're not going to win enough football games in this league, and that's the problem we had today."
–Sam Rutigliano, Browns coach


"I won't know until my barber tells me on Monday."
–Knute Rockne, when asked why Notre Dame lost a game


"At least I'm not a stockbroker."
–Watson Brown, Vanderbilt coach, on a bad loss (which occurred the same week as the stock market crash)


"If it was, Army and Navy would be playing for the national championship every year."
–Bobby Bowden, when asked if discipline was the key to winning


"They say losing builds character. I have all the character I need."
–Ray Malavasi, Rams and Broncos coach


"I feel like the guy in the javelin competition who won the toss and elected to receive."
–Mack Brown, Tulane coach, on his team's 1-3 start

"When you're winning, you don't need any friends. When you're losing, you don't have any friends anyway."
–Woody Hayes

"I think it's a good idea."
–John McKay, Buccaneers coach, when asked about his team's execution after a loss

"Our defensive backs were like a river. There was a lot more activity at the mouth than at the source."
–Mike Baab, Browns center, on his team's secondary

"Hindsight is always 50-50."
–Cam Newton, after a Panthers-Bengals overtime tie

"My only feeling about superstition is that it's unlucky to be behind at the end of the game."
–Duffy Daugherty, Michigan State coach

"I'm not allowed to comment on lousy officiating."
–Jim Finks, Saints GM

"It makes it easy when you've got a defense out there playing."
–Carson Palmer, complimenting the Bengals "defense" after a 58-48 win

"As the famous artist Vincent van Gogh would say, 'Gang, it wasn't a masterpiece, but it will sell.'"
–Mike Ditka, after a Bears victory

"I wish I could remember my halftime speech so I could forget it."
–Jerry Davitch, Idaho football coach, on blowing a halftime lead and losing big

"You don't think I don't think they don't think about the bowl game?"
–Ron Zook, Illinois football coach, on his pep talk before a loss to Minnesota

"The people who do those stats, half the time they're spilling ketchup on themselves and trying to wipe it off."
–Jason Taylor, disagreeing with stats that showed he had no tackles in a game

"We're still shooting ourselves in the mouth."
–Marcel West, Alabama wide receiver, on his team's mistakes

"I'm going to study Spanish so I can use a few expletives in my press conferences next season."
–Francis Peay, Northwestern coach

"I'm really happy for Coach Cooper and the guys who've been around here for six or seven years, especially our seniors."
–Bob Hoying, Ohio State quarterback, after winning a Big Ten title

"I give the same halftime speech over and over. It works best when my players are better than the other coach's players."
–Chuck Mills, Wake Forest coach

"A stick of gum would have been enough."
–Fred Biletnikoff, Raiders wide receiver, as he was awarded his Super Bowl XI MVP trophy

"We seem to attract our own."
–Chuck Noll, Steelers coach, when a sewer pipe burst in the locker room after a bad loss

"It's so quiet, you could hear a sweat sock drop."
–Marv Levy, Bills coach, on the Buffalo locker room after losing Super Bowl XXVI

"It's too soon after the car wreck to say we're feeling better."
–Marv Levy, meeting with his team after their fourth straight Super Bowl loss